There's more to Life than a house in Goa

There's more to Life than a house in Goa

HETA PANDIT

With a foreword by
Dr Nina Sabnani and Wendell Rodricks

PARTRIDGE
A Penguin Random House Company

ISBN: Hardcover   978-1-4828-5717-7
           Softcover   978-1-4828-5716-0
           eBook   978-1-4828-5715-3

Print information available on the last page.

To order additional copies of this book, contact
Partridge India
000 800 10062 62
orders.india@partridgepublishing.com

www.partridgepublishing.com/india

Contents

Foreword

by Wendell Rodricks

E ver since I knew Heta Pandit, I was astonished and pleased that a lady with so much passion was gifted to Goa. There are many people who arrive in Goa, fall instantly in love with the Iberian flavour and then set about buying a house... their piece of paradise in a heavenly land. It is almost always a given. After a few days in one of India's smallest state, house guests and perfect strangers pop the question. "Can we buy a house here?" This is perplexing yet not surprising. Everyone wants a piece of India's golden state.

Most create a bubble of an ideal house (not home), put up high walls, enjoy a magnificent view and are content to have "the Goa house". This is after the Delhi farm house of the 90's. The Goa house soon lost lustre in the 2000's to the Dubai, Singapore, London; Manhattan houses ("so much surplus cash, why buy in Mumbai when overseas is cheaper?").

But Heta was different. Always. Especially when you read this story. Hidden jewels of a personality largely unknown. Inheritor of three houses (Can I steal her Mom and get bequeathed the same?). Author of many books... all epicentred on houses.

It was Heta's Goa house that surprised me. It lay wedged between a winding road and many houses. It looked like it was impossibly inviting people or a vehicle to plough in. Literally. I gawked, gasped and gave it up to 'insanity'; a Parsi trait that obviously Heta inherited.

To people I asked rather undiplomatically "Is that really Heta Pandit's Goa house?" they nodded in resigned despair.

Honestly...here is a lady who went out on a limb where few 'outsiders' go. She began the Goa Heritage Action Group, reviving the ethos of Fontainhas in a one dramatic sweep, identified heritage buildings and homes, negotiated with politicians and administrators with charm, wrote passionately about Goa's working hands, heritage walking tours and celestial objects of architectural delight. And while I always presumed she might have an architectural Goan jewel hidden away, I realized that this was her first Goan house. My respect soared.

For many reasons.

This is different. A paradigm shift of desire.

People normally buy a house first. When the house is all gleaming and quasi -Goan in flavour, they then begin to contemplate... to decide what to do in Goa. 'Do we mix with the locals? Do we care about the garbage situation? Why care about the village or state when we can create our own Goa? Goans considers us outsiders anyway...so let's just stay away from their local issues and live in peace with everyone.'

Heta Pandit put the cart before the horse. The causes before the house.

The causes before the house? THAT is revolutionary.

And that is the very reason you should read this book.

Quite simply because there is more to Heta than ...Heta Pandit, the name and persona.

Now finally here is a book on Heta herself. In her words. In her selective confessions. Did you know these aspects of Heta Pandit? That she worked with Jane Goodall in Tanzania at a chimpanzee research station. That she is India's first woman Assistant Tea Estate Manager? The mind boggles. It boggles even more at the dramatic change of residences across many vistas. Along the way we meet family, make friends and rejoice in a truly unconventional life.

All through this remarkable journey we do not lose the vision of a benign, ever smiling, always positive Heta Pandit. This book puts many things into perspective about a lady I have admired from the onset, ever since she arrived in Goa. This is her life, and what a journey it has been.

There truly is more to life than a house in Goa.

Wendell Rodricks,
Fashion Designer, Writer, Environmental Activist.

Also by Heta Pandit

To Mana

Foreword

There's more to Life than a House in Goa is a remarkable account of a full life, told with warmth, wit, and a scorching honesty that brings one to one's feet with respect and affection for the author. Houses, forests, beaches, and aimless wanderings merge with strong positions against authority, concern for the environment, and a will to do and be.

One wonders how can one person have lived all those lives?

We travel with Heta from one life to another, from Baroda, Bombay, and Goa to London, Tanzania, and the tea gardens of Munnar, and each life seamlessly takes over at a pace that varies with the events. From moving fast and even leaving us to imagine the rest she moves ever so slowly, in no hurry to get to the point as she lovingly lingers on details, whether it is a walk in the jungle, the landlord in Goa, or the life in Siganpore.

Through the pages, one can feel the strong presence of the mother figure that is acknowledged with love, respect, pride, and a bit of awe. Couched in the folds of family history and life events are subtle insights into struggles for identity, of being a part of a community, be it work or religious, of being a woman and making sense of life as it unfolds.

Not being able to put it down till one reaches the end of the book, one would marvel as a friend: there's more to Heta than meets the eye! Can anyone surprise you and make you smile as much? She does!

Dr Nina Sabnani
Professor, Industrial Design Centre
Indian Institute of Technology
Mumbai

Preface

I simply can't talk about anything but houses. Is it because I own four historic homes in India? Three out of four are in different towns. Three out of four I inherited from my mother. I purchased one in Goa in 2006 and yet consider myself the previous owner's spiritual heir. Long before I inherited these homes, I began writing about houses. I actively advocate preservation. How did this happen? It's a long story, a story I'm obsessed with. Friends complain that I hardly talk of anything else. All my conversations revolve around the houses, their upkeep, their leaking roofs, their Minton floors, their refurbishments, their stories, and the spirits that inhabit them. I had to write all these stories down. Naturally, my own story is part of the story of these houses. I have written about other peoples' houses in Goa. It's time I write about my own houses, the one in Mumbai, the two in Panchgani, and the one in Goa that I love best. It's time to talk personal history. It's time to recall family values. It's time to remember the way things were. After all, the stories of the houses are also the stories of the people that inhabit them. It's time to think that there's more to life than a house in Goa.

Acknowledgements

This book, and indeed my whole life, would not have been what it is if it had not been for my mother's support through all my trials and tribulations. With me still, in spirit, my thanks go to her. My thanks also go to Vinayak Nayak, friend and executive editor of the magazine *Goa Today* for the permission to reproduce some of the articles I had done for the magazine for use as material for the book. I thank my assistant Tanjul Sharma for her youthful inputs and enthusiastic contributions and to Farrina Gailey at Partridge for her encouragement and patience. Most of all, my thanks go to all my friends and all the members of my family: Dhunrumi, Yasmin, Rustom, Dilshad, Rushad, Tiyana and Vivaan, Jena, Rahul, Siddharth, Noshir, Maya, Diana, Aspi, and Minu and Farhad for making life full of fun and self-worth. Thanks go to Rahul for taking pains over the Pallonji family tree and adding names of the girls in the family. Grateful thanks to friend and mentor Chandrima Pal for her helpful advice. Thanks to my friend and colleague Tushar Rao for taking fresh photographs of the houses in Mumbai, Panchgani and Goa. And last of all thanks to Rahul for getting so irritated with my constant nattering about the Goa house thereby giving me the title for the book.

I

A House in Goa

'Number 54 . . . house with a bamboo door . . . House of Bamboo . . .'

As fate would have it, Goa drew me in more than two decades ago, but it took a blessing from the gods for me to find a home. Mum knew that I would have enough houses to live in after she had gone. She still wanted me to have a house of my own. 'If your heart is set on Goa', she said, 'you need a house here.' After so many years in Goa, perhaps it was time to drop anchor, I thought.

For those of us who believe it, everything in life is preordained. Why else would I have been caught in the 1993 communal riots in Mumbai, been terrified of being asked if I was Hindu or Muslim (I am neither and I am both) from that year onwards and deciding to move out of Mumbai supposedly never to return? 'The personality of the metropolis has changed,' I told my friends and family when I left. 'I am going to a place where I can be closer to nature away from the bestial expressions of the building burning and decapitating desires of men and women.'

After years of allowing destiny to lead me by the hand (and head), I thought I was the mistress of my own destiny finally. A year and a half after being close to nature in the tea gardens of Munnar, Kerala, I found myself upside-down on its precipitous mountain tracks hit by a jeep packed to the floorboards with people, a goat, and a few sacks of tamarind. My motorcycle made it without so much as a scratch, but I had to undergo surgery and have a bag strapped to my leg to collect fluid and bear the scars of twenty-four stitches for the rest of my life. I had been sewn up with ordinary black sewing thread in India's best industrial hospital.

Never quite sure if Goa would be a permanent home, my cousin Mahrukh and I lived at a friend's flat in Colva, then rented a one room terrace flat at Varca, then a single-bedroom apartment in Mapusa, and then a farmhouse in Guirim, a 500-square-foot basement flat with seven windows in Porvorim, all completely and totally diverse from the beautiful historic heritage houses in Goa that I am writing about. 'You're taking vicarious pleasure in other people's houses because you don't have a home of your own here in Goa' came from a prominent Goan writer whom I visited one afternoon. The comment hit home where it came to rest, but it was not at peace.

After eleven years of being a guest in Goa, I now wanted a home of my own. My family owned a heritage house in Bandra, Mumbai. It completed its 101st year in 2015. Mum went to school in Panchgani. Her father had bought her a house just across the school gates. The bungalow and cottage will complete a century in a year from now. Then there is the ancestral house built in 1903 in Gujarat; it was built single-handedly by my mother's paternal aunt in the absence of the men who were always away on business. Why would I want to add to this collection of houses? As they say, common sense is a beast. An unreasonable desire made me begin my search for a house in Goa. I called in a broker and expected him to produce a house for me.

Eleven years in Goa and with all the work I had done on houses, it shouldn't have been difficult. A whole year and twenty-four houses viewed and nothing really suitable turned up. If the houses were there, there were no staff quarters. If the garage and garden were perfect, the house was loopy. If everything was perfect, there was no access road to the house. If house, garden, garage, and the lions on the gateposts were perfect, the papers were not. It was time to burst into tears of frustration, and that's exactly what I did.

'Goa does not want me to have a house here. I am now sure of it,' I cried to a friend. 'Listen', he said, 'I know you don't believe in these things, but there is a priest that I consult before taking important business decisions. Will you take this one last shot at it before you call it quits?' There was at least one Goan in Goa who was keen that I have a house here. I decided to give it a try and went off on this long and winding journey to a remote temple in Ponda. I met the soothsayer, trying very hard to hide my cynicism. The soothsayer asked me what my date of birth was, stationed me on a wooden bench in the temple, and went for a long walk. Bewildered and certain that this wild goose chase would get me nowhere, I waited with the car keys ready for a quick flight.

The old priest came back from his round of the temple grounds and asked rather absently, 'Uh, what was it that you had come for? Marriage is not on the cards.'

'I had known that a long time ago,' I told him, now really annoyed. I told him I had come to ask him if I would ever find a house. 'Oh? House?' he asked. 'What was your date of birth again?' I gave it to him in a loud impatient voice. '25 August 1954'. He snapped his fingers, turned around, and began to hum softly. I couldn't believe my ears. The temple priest was singing to the temple walls. 'Number 54 . . . house with a bamboo door . . . House of Bamboo . . .' *Things could certainly get interesting around here*, I thought. He came back, patted me on the head, and said, 'You'll get your house on your birthday.' I thanked him, left a token in the temple box, and made my way back to my basement flat in Porvorim, even more depressed than before. My birthday was ten days away.

I was enjoying a leisurely birthday breakfast with some friends when I got a call from my broker Sanjiv, who said, 'Drop everything you are doing and come to Saligao. I have got you your house.' I literally dropped my fork, dashed into the car, and drove to Saligao where Sanjiv was waiting for me. I only had to open the car door and I knew. I knew I had found my house. In retrospect, I think the house found me. It did not matter that I did not have the keys to the house. It did not matter that I had to stand on my toes on the moulding and look through the chinks to see the flooring. It did not matter that the living room corner of the house jutted out on the road at a crazy angle. It did not matter that the village road had sliced the house, garage, and staff room into two unequal halves. It just did not matter.

This story is nine years old now, and I can never forget that I had found my house on my birthday just as the Goa gods had preordained. It had been a family tradition to name houses after the women of the house. Our Bandra home is called Tehmi Terrace, after my grandmother Tehmina. Another house my grandfather owned in Dadar was called Khorshed Abad after Khorshedbanoo, my grandmother's other name. The main bungalow in Panchgani is called Dhun-Heta, the cottage across the garden named Jena, after my sister. I named the Goa house after my niece, my sister's daughter, Maia, tweaking the spelling slightly. Mai is also another word for mother in Goa's native Konkani, a language that speaks of a mother's all-encompassing love. For me, her laboured passing away.

Most people know with what difficulty I got myself a house in Goa. Having got it, most people also know that I had to do it up to make it habitable at a considerable expense. The previous owner of the house had passed on ten years before I bought the house, and the house had not been lived in since then. Sonny had been a bachelor with very few wants and practically no social life. The whole house had one light bulb in it and his sanitary habits were a huge question mark. I thought I might be able to defray the costs of the restoration by keeping the house open to visitors at a small guest charge.

How difficult could that be? Goa was a tourist destination; the nearest beach was only eight kilometre away. I was on the 'short-cut' to the Saturday Night Markets at Arpora. Besides, the house jutted out so precariously on to the road that you didn't really have to look for it. It was in everyone's eye. Most taxi drivers who brought visitors in knew it as the 'corner house'. I began to take in guests, people recommended by the people I had known in Mumbai, Pune, and Delhi.

My first guests were naturally from Mumbai, a city that I had come from and had many friends. There was a lovely large family that stayed with us once. They were good fun-loving people with members of the family varying in size, shape, and age. One of the little ones spilt some milk on the sofa and my cook and caretaker reminded them that they would have to pay for the damage. 'We've paid a rent for our stay. For three days, your house is ours. We can do what we like here.' That was that. The guests stayed on, my cook left.

Some members of my extended family came as my guests. After they left, the staff found some rather interesting packets on the dresser obviously left behind by mistake. That much white powder in the packets would have had my staff of Nepali boys dancing to a lifetime of no music. That is when I decided that I would put a stop to friends of friends from the rest of India. I had guests from Europe, a very nice family of five, three children and two adults. When they were about to leave, I checked the rooms to see if they had forgotten anything. All the mattresses had been stripped of their bed linen and the mattresses were standing up against the wall. Had they all slept standing up?

Another guest from Germany arrived with a lady he called his wife. My Nepali houseboy refused to enter the house after that. The lady did not speak a word of English or German. In fact, she did not even speak any Russian. All she did was giggle and laugh and run around from one room to another sometimes forgetful of the fact that one needed to be dressed. That didn't bother me so much really. I mean. It is hot in Goa, right? What did bother me was the number of huge dish antennas in my living room. Apparently, the German guest had just shut his office down in Delhi and had moved to Goa to set up business here. I did not want to ask him what the nature of his business might be.

After having these rather curious guests, I decided not to open the house anymore. Then I had an appeal from a friend of a friend of a friend pleading that I consider taking in an elderly, very respectable couple from somewhere around Delhi. *Well, what harm could an elderly couple do?* I thought. They were really polite when they arrived. They both had impeccable manners and impeccable taste in luggage. Unfortunately, somebody forgot to tell me that the poor lady was incontinent. Whenever I visited my own house, there were drops of bodily fluids on the floor and both the bathrooms were in an unmentionable condition. All the mattresses had to be changed after they left, all the toilet seats replaced, and the carpets sent to the dry cleaners.

Then Mum got seriously ill and I had to move to Mumbai so I began to look for a tenant who could rent the house on a long-term basis. A friend was to take the house and I thanked the stars for my good fortune. Unfortunately, however, a few days before she was to move in, her circumstances changed dramatically and I was in a crisis. Five brokers were called in, several friends asked to 'spread the word', but I did not meet with any success. In the meanwhile, the crisis in Mumbai got worse. Finally, I got the lovely Mandira, a therapist, to rent the house and three years passed in absolute bliss. Mandira is now a friend for life!

True to form, I asked my friend to leave the house after a three year stay. This was out of the illogical fear that if a tenant stayed on for too long, there would be some 'Bombay type' trouble and that she would not leave without a fight. I haven't regretted a decision as much as I did, asking Mandira to leave. Mum was still seriously ill, and I had to look for a new set of tenants. Facebook came to the rescue or so, I thought. I found this Irish couple, both chefs. They seemed kosher enough when I went to see them at their place in Mumbai and nothing seemed amiss. After they moved into the house in Goa, I would visit once a month and everything seemed fine then too. I must have so wanted them to be fine that I did not look at what I was supposed to look. Why did I not notice that the notepad on the dining table was open at exactly the same page on every visit? That the laptop and the printers and fax machines were all duds?

Why did I not figure out why the bedroom doors were shut tight each time I came to say hello? When they gave the house back, all my antique furniture had been thrown in the garage, one piece piled on top of the other, the garden had been laid bare, the cooking range still had blackened cake batter stuck in it, and the bougainvillea had overgrown so badly that there was no back garden left. The water tanks had to be cleaned and all the plumbing had to be replaced because the pipes were choked with monsoon mud. It did not look as if anyone had even lived there for years. The house had been a stage set on my visits.

But somebody had been living there. I got a phone call from the police station a couple of months ago. 'Did I know anyone named Tara D'Souza? A model?' That lady had given my house as her permanent address. 'I had not rented the house to any Tara D'Souza,' I said and then remembered that I had emptied out a whole chest of drawers filled with strings after the Irish couple had stayed. 'What company or brand did this Tara D'Souza model for? Victoria's Secret?'

II

Growing Up with Mother

'We are different. We are Parsis. We have a car. Our mother speaks English.'

It is the winter of 2014 and I am trying very hard to fit into my mother's socks. Slipping into her shoes was easy. Not so her socks. How many people wear textured socks, with treads at the soles to stop you from falling, I wonder. The socks have been stashed away in a wooden cupboard for thirty years. The label from a Flea Market in London is still intact. I peel the old label off, and the two stitches that hold the toes of the socks together fall at my feet. I look down at my toes. I stare at these little animals that my feet have magically produced without my knowledge. They hold me mesmerized for hours at a stretch. The floor is cold and speckled with marble chips on a smooth unwrinkled bed of cement, the kind that is neatly cut into squares, laid out, and then walked upon while everyone pretends not to see the joints that show up in between.

Mine were not pretty lady's toes by any standard. In fact, they were long and narrow and the knobs they had on them were a constant source of embarrassment. I would often fold them in to hide them from prying eyes as I was convinced that they were so ugly that people could see my toes long before they could see me. I also had very long and narrow feet. I often wished that my feet were the size of the foot after the toes were curled in. That to me was the ideal-sized foot: small, narrow, covered with a thin film of white skin at the bottom, and a golden coffee-brown unblemished film over the top and soft to touch and white. That would be the perfect foot. Instead, I had to compromise with browned toes with both calluses and character.

Each of my toenails had a personality of its own. The big toe on the left foot was always neat and trimmed and geometrically squared off at the top. It could have been the innocent face of a crocodile by a placid lake, not its menacing whip-like tail. It was quite what I wanted out of life then – a sense of order, quick reflexes, and an innocent face behind an ambitious tenacious mind with razor-sharp teeth ready for a kill. I wished! The big toe on the right foot, however, was who I really was. It caused me acute sorrow as it changed shape from day to day. It curled in shyness, crossed over the other toes when I wanted to go to the toilet, and curled inside my shoe just before I began to speak. That big toe caused me some concern. And not just in shoe shops where shoe salesmen understand the shapes of toes, the fatness of heels, and the burning tongues of bunions to come.

Your right foot is not who you want to be but who you really are. The left foot is who you would really like to be. I know it's a theory, but it's true, really. The first toe on my right foot built in the same classical lines was in fact slightly over the big toe in thickness and in length but looked more like a half moon with the bottom bitten off where pieces of skin were taking over territory they had once lost in a long-forgotten battle. Then there were the other two third toes, their nails in a fixed unbending triangle. These toes bounced up from where they were supposed to be tucked in quiet along with others. That is because I was born, my mother said to me once, with non-aligned toes. The third toe had grown one level above the rest and that for a girl was awful. So mother had pressed these two errant toes down with the flat bottom of a stainless-steel bowl dipped in cooking oil. It worked. The toes slid down to be in plane with the others except in times of stress or while trying out new shoes. I still tend to buy shoes that are one size too small for me.

At 32, still conscious of my Parsi nose

I wish mother had also done something about my Parsi nose. The toes had been kept in line but the nose stayed and so have the last little toes.

Until I was thirty-two years old, the little toes were only as big as small shirt buttons. That is all one could see of them, I mean. Whatever mass fell out of the button size and shape went neatly tucked in and squared off under the rest of my feet. A fried prawn would have been a prettier sight. Those were my shy and reticent toes, an indicator of my being at that age. They're coming out now, at sixty, coming of age.

That probably explains why I write in my sleep. That is the only time that I cannot see my toes and get distracted by their off-putting shapes. The irony of it is that it is my toes that start tingling when I want to write; it is they who set the alarm bells ringing. At first bell, vibrations creep up the flat of my feet and end up at the ankles. I twist my ankles and the tingling moves sideways finding a passageway up the thick fat trunks of my Parsi thighs. Then the knees, bent over on a hard pillow, straighten themselves out, and I begin to write.

Before I write, however, I have to be in the right shape myself. My bedclothes, my hair, my slippers by the bed have to be in the right shape too. This is important because I carry a bin in my head and have to pull out ideas and words from the bin one by one. If the thought or word is the wrong shape and size, it has to be put away and another pulled out. The bin has locks on all sides. The trick is then to find an opening in the outer wall of this bin and spin the outer wall so that the inner wall and outer wall are both aligned. It is tricky business, noisy too, sometimes squeaky, with rusty ball bearings turning slowly in my head.

One had to hold the bin open until the words spilled out, one after the other and tumbled on to paper. You had to do this whole thing really quickly before the bin combinations went askew and the whole thing self detonated or slammed shut. What was more the danger was that the bin emptied itself, with no help from me and all the ideas, thoughts, and words lay scattered unchecked on the floor, on the walls and thrown around the bed, the bedclothes, my slippers, under my curling toes. Nothing can be worse than when you try to pull back spilled words with your toes, especially if those toes were the way they were, turned this way, and that resembling unsalted cold boiled potato that had neither taste nor smell.

Finding thirty-year old socks with the label intact came as no surprise. Everything that had been bought on Mother's first trip to England in 1972 was special. Nothing in our house ever got thrown away even after it was worn to shreds. What most mothers called rubbish, my mother stowed away in large black tin trunks and old leather suitcases that her parents had brought back from various ship voyages from and to the sea port of Aden in the 1930s. Into these rotting old suitcases went broken dolls, old exercise books, personality-altering 'handwriting' copy books and needlework done by all of us at some pin prick stage in our school lives. While I was out with my school friends in the lacy henna-hedged compound fences of the officers colony where we lived in Baroda and weaving dreams of becoming somebody someday soon, my mother was doing her life's work with our neighbour Mrs Deshpande. She was trying to convince the homely lady who had two daughters of her own to steer them towards a career instead of relying on crotchet and good husbands to ensure a good hold on the future.

I would often take my needlework home to 'Deshpande Aunty' to finish. What would take her half an hour at a leisurely pace would have taken me weeks of mental and physical torture. Her short, grime-ingested fingernails would get to work almost immediately, compulsively unwinding the crotchet thread from its reel and onto her fat, arched thumb. Before I had turned eleven, I had got my first lesson in management. 'If you can get someone else to do it for you, don't do it yourself.' All those doilies and cushion covers, patchwork quilts for babies and embroidered shopping bags for mummies went into the tin trunks, usurping as 'Heta's needlework'. Mother was so proud of my accomplishments at school. She chose to ignore 'Deshpande Aunty' swishing around in her cotton saree and thick white cotton blouse, her large breasts freed of constricting factory-made bras, her fingers forever moving, moving, moving over casting *jalebis*, folding *samosas*, rolling out *rotis*, and finishing my needlework.

Officers Colony, the Baroda house

As collections went, most of what went into the trunks was worthless. To my mother, it meant the whole world. She would refer to is as *samaan*, stuff. There was the iron *samaan*, the old *samaan*, Grandma's *samaan*, the *samaan* in the loft which was mostly newspapers and magazines assembled over ten years at least and always referred to as 'new'. The newspapers and magazines were never stacked neatly but left strewn around the loft so that we could dive into them at short notice for school projects and scrapbooks. Somehow, we always seemed to find what we were looking for. If the newspapers and magazines were nibbled away by the rats in the loft or covered in cockroach carapaces, we did not notice. To us, they were crackling new.

Then there was the *kitchen samaan* and the *gaadi samaan* that seemed to be interchangeable. Or so it seemed to us because the kitchen *samaan* would often end up in the garage and car *samaan* in the kitchen on the top-most shelves where none of us could reach. If someone was giving away a prize for household junk or goods collected over three generations, we would have won the contest hands down. What were my earliest memories as a child? I'd put 'Moms are sweet and comforting' and 'Dads are scary' on the top of the list. Dads do very important work we were told. As children, we were instructed to take off our slippers when Dad got home from work. Flip-flops made a flipping-flopping sound as one scampered around the house and that disturbed Dad after a hard day at the office. The other most important message was that we were different. 'We are different. We are Parsis. We have a car. Our mother speaks English.'

You could only speak to Dad when you were spoken to and on Sundays. Important work at the office always had him in a bad mood. I would run to where all the slippers were and get him his slippers as soon as he had taken off his office shoes. Nothing else would please him. Dad also had high expectations from all his children, even higher from my brother Dhunrumi because he was a boy. When I was five, I learnt that we had a Grandmother and that she did not like us. Mum and Dad would leave us with various 'aunties and uncles' to rush off to the Bombay High Court where they were fighting a case against Grandma. I did not understand what property meant until I was a full seven. And then Jena was born (they were playing *Chaudvi ka chand ho* on the radio when we went to see her at the hospital), and she became my new doll, my baby sister. When D and I first saw her, we were appalled. Was this humanoid-like creature really our sister? There was some white gossamer stuff on her that looked like cobwebs, and besides, she did not seem to have any lips.

There was something else that happened. When I was eleven, I woke up one morning with a huge blood stain in my underwear. I had no doubt hurt myself while playing at school. Mum would be annoyed, so I just pulled on another pair of cotton panties over the stained ones and held both my thighs tight. The bleeding would not stop. I plucked up courage and called my mother into the toilet to see. Much to my surprise she was not annoyed at all. She seemed thrilled. She gave me a tight hug and then ran out of the toilet. I sat there, bewildered and full of the trepidation. While I was there, Mother had cut up her old duster coat and had come with a wad made of the rough coarse fabric printed with red and yellow flowers. I tucked it in between my thighs and it felt more uncomfortable than I had ever been.

'Heta has grown up now, dear,' she whispered to Dad when he got home from his important work at the office that evening. He was holding me up high in his arms in an embrace when he heard her. He dropped me on the floor that very instant. *I am no longer his little girl*, I thought, *something must have happened.* He never touched me after that day, and I stopped running to get him his slippers.

III

Mixed Heritage

'Mummy, Daddy, this is Patrick (or Sunil or Jaffer), and I am going to marry him.'

People often ask me how my parents met. It is an innocuous question except when you have one parent who is a Parsi Zoroastrian and the other who is not. Most Parsis I know socialise only with their own kind, and I mean their own kind of Parsi. Parsi music lovers fraternise with other Parsi music lovers, Parsi lovers of good food with other Parsi gourmands. So it is a source of grave concern and great curiosity when you hear of a particular Parsi woman (in this case my mother) meeting, falling in love, and marrying a 'non-Parsi', an 'outsider', my non-Parsi father. For having done that, she is forever known as 'that one who married out' or the 'outmarried one'.

Unless the rules have changed since this writing has gone to print, Parsi women are severely chastised by their fellow community members, not allowed into the hallowed grounds, lands, and prayer halls of the zealously guarded fire temples and not given any kind of religious rites when they die. The children of this mixed heritage are stigmatised for no fault of their own and the mix in their genes frowned upon with suspicion. Most Parsi Zoroastrian parents, therefore, live in mortal dread of the day when one of their children will walk into the house with a future partner in tow and say something like 'Mummy, Daddy, this is Patrick (or Sunil or Jaffer), and I am going to marry him'.

So as a precaution, most Parsi parents will forbid their pure-blooded offspring from fraternising with the *parjaats,* the 'nons' to minimize the chances of such dreaded events. I would not blame them really. The punishing outcome of being ostracized by the community is severe. When my mother decided to marry my father, her parents were so horrified that their only child was to marry a 'non' that while my father was away in the United States getting a degree from the Texas University and Mum was with her parents alone, they locked her up in the two-terraced rooms in our Bandra house and forced her into marrying an elderly friend of the family, a pauper nonetheless but a Parsi. She stayed married to this man for a while, even changing her last name to his as was customary. When my father returned from the United States, the lovers met in secret and my feisty mother, always a rebel, got her marriage annulled and married my father.

All hell broke loose. Her parents refused to speak to her, and a month before I was born, her father died of a massive heart attack, a heartbroken man. This left us, my mother and me, her first-born, bearing the guilt of this loss all our lives. Bereft of some of the property that had been willed to the daughter by a generous and forgiving father, Mum's enraged mother Tehmina threatened to disown her, saying, '*Hoon dhani ni dhaniyani tu kaun?*' which would translate roughly as 'I am the widow of the owner, the wife of the husband, and I refuse to acknowledge you anymore'. This rather harsh tirade coming from your own grandmother both puzzled and hurt us as children. I must have been about twelve years old when I first heard it. In any case our grandmother Tehmina was a complete stranger to us for most of our childhood.

Tehmina, like all my mother's aunts, uncles, and first cousins from both sides of the family (barring one cousin in Nagpur) had refused to have anything to do with us simply because our father was a 'non'. Mum would often speak of her father, our grandfather Rustomjee, having six brothers, two sisters, and of our great-grandfather Pallonjee, having married his first cousin (a preference we were told 'to keep the money in the family'). There should have been, therefore, lots of relatives. We, of course, did not see any of them.

To add to our confusion and a sort of 'in the shadows existence', there would be the odd visit from some stranger who turned out to be related to us in some way. Largely ignored, we would only be part of family drama when this stranger said something rude to my mother or to us directly. 'What have you gone and done? Who have you latched yourself to? The soles of my feet are fairer and more beautiful than you and your children' is one example that I remember quite clearly. As we grew older, we learnt who that stranger (later a frequent visitor to my grandmother's house) was. He was my grandmother's brother's son, my mother's first cousin, and someone who had been promised all the family wealth by my grandmother.

I first heard I had a grandmother when I was about five years old and my brother was three. Grandma had refused to have anything to do with my parents, and so one of my mother's closest friends Najoo decided to smuggle us in and introduce her to her only grandchildren. 'Najoo Aunty' would often stand in for my mother if mother had errands to do outside the house. One day, she simply grabbed us by the hand and took us to the Bandra house. We went into this large house, painted pink on the outside and yellow on the inside, and sat on a large sofa, the only piece of furniture in the capacious living room. I remember pulling the hem of my dress down to cover my knees as I sat on the edge of the sofa because I had been told to 'sit like a lady'. My brother, who had just turned three, began to pretend he was in the middle of a swimming pool and started waving his legs and arms about. We had no idea who we had come to see.

We visit Grandma at the Bandra house

We had also just begun to read, and this house obviously had someone who loved newspapers. Every stick of furniture was, from our vertically challenged point of view, covered in newspapers. We had never seen so many copies of the *Jam-e-Jamshed* before in our lives. Come to think of it, we had never seen a Gujarati paper before this. The Mutt and Jeff cartoons in the *Jame* caught my eye as we waited for this mysterious person to emerge. I was too young to appreciate the humour but that was the only thing that looked familiar to me. The entire newspaper used to be in Gujarati except for the cartoon strip. Both my brother and I did a few flip-flops over the tables, chairs, and window sills, spreading ourselves silly, to try and read the Roman script and make sense of what looked like a ridiculous cartoon strip.

Grandma swept into the room in a green-printed *gavan,* house gown, a familiar garment to most Parsi women. She was wearing soft black house slippers called *sapat* (after the Portuguese *sapatas*). A diminutive woman, complexion like whipped cream and a grim look on her face, is what I remember of her from that day. She looked us up and down, and we giggled nervously. She then turned to 'Najoo Aunty' and asked, '*Bhanta sikhavyouch key?*' Have they been taught how to say their prayers? Before 'Najoo Aunty' could answer, my three year-old brother replied, 'Yes, I go to college.' Grandma burst out laughing. We were amazed. This lady we had come to see did not have a single tooth in her mouth! I have no idea what transpired between my estranged mother, our grandmother, and 'Najoo Aunty' after that day, but our lessons in the Zend Avesta began soon after that.

Until then, both our parents had brought us up to think we were Indian first and Hindu/Muslim/Parsi/Christian/Sikh after. India had won its independence from British colonial rule not very long ago, and patriotic feelings ran through every liberal-minded Indian home. Neither of our parents was too religious for their own good. At four, I was sent to the Gujarati-medium kindergarten in Poona in what was then Bombay Presidency. Our parents had friends and neighbours who were Hindu, Parsi, and Christian. In the absence of relatives, our neighbours and friends fulfilled the role of 'aunties and uncles', and their children became our friends and surrogate cousins. When anyone asked us what 'caste' we were, we were told to stand erect and swell our chests to say, 'INDIAN'. Even so, I remember several incidents when I was teased at kindergarten for being a *bawa*, the derogatory term for a Parsi.

Children can be cruel. If some child broke wind in the kindergarten, the others would pick on me, pointing a finger, and scream '*Aada paada kaun paada bawaji ka beta paada*' which in English would be something like 'Ina Mina Myna mo, who's farting in the store? It has to be the Parsi kiddo.' The hurt and humiliation of this victimisation added more confusion to issues of identity. Were we Parsis then? Why did my classmates call me *bawaji ka beta*? No one I knew had ever called my dad a *bawaji*. Besides, I was not a *beta*, a son. Wasn't I a *beti*, a daughter?

When Bombay Presidency was bifurcated into Gujarat and Maharashtra in 1960, my Gujarati-speaking father had to accept an order to move to the new state of Gujarat. My mother was anxious and did not want to leave the city where she had made her first home and let go of all the people who had supported her during her trying years. I was nearly six years old and enjoyed the excitement of moving into the colony with twenty government-style quarters with other government employee families. My mother derided her Gujarati vegetarian neighbours and called them, '*Patli dhal khavawala*', meaning 'They who slurp thin *dhal*.' Our *dhal* at home was high on consistency and packed with meat. So now we knew why Mother was so reluctant to move from Poona. In our neighbours' kitchens, there was no meat. Now we knew we were different. Now we knew why our neighbours' children were allowed to play with us but were forbidden to eat anything off our table or even have a glass of water at our place. 'The glasses in your house smell of egg. Your water is contaminated,' they told us plainly. 'You eat meat. You are non-vegetarians.' We were in a different 'non' category once again.

For the next few years, we oscillated in a sort of twilight zone as far as faith and religion were concerned. There were no other Parsi families in the colony except when I got to my teens. Our nearest neighbours were the Deshpande family and the derogatory term for a Gujarati, 'Gujju' had not yet been invented. My mother's closest friend in the colony was, therefore, Mrs Deshpande, a Poona Brahmin who could not speak Gujarati and did not consider her Gujarati neighbours deserving of her company. I cannot say this for certain, but I think my mother felt intimidated by the other Parsi families in the city and kept her distance from them for fear of being insulted for marrying 'outside'. Except for the few Parsi school friends that we would bring home occasionally and our liberal-minded *agiary* temple priest Dasturji Maneksha, there was no contact with the town Parsis. Mrs Deshpande and her four children took us under their wing. We were introduced to good Poona Marathi, taught how to finish off a meal with *dahi bhath,* curd and rice or *doodh bhat,* milk and rice with a generous sprinkling of sugar on top, and how to conduct a *Ganesh arti,* a votive offering to Lord Ganesha.

Ironically, just as our Gujarati neighbours held a prejudice against us for being 'meat-eating Parsis', they also revered Mother for being proficient in the English language. They would come to her for help with their homework in what they called 'the second language'. With just twenty families to interact with, our colony life soon became that of an extended family. In the absence of any contact with relatives or members of the Parsi community in our small town, our neighbours became family. We were in and out of their homes, joining them in washing their Hindu idols in milk and water, rolling *papads* with them, pickling mangoes with them, and slurping up their *patli dhal*.

Mother, on the other hand, was doing her utmost to show us (and them) that we were different. She trooped us off once a week to the wholesale market to buy tomatoes when they were cheap and then marched us into a marathon 'tomato ketchup making season'. Our neighbours had never seen ketchup. She sent us off with English-style 'porridge' for breakfast every morning and had a man pick us up from the school bus stop like we were princesses. Our first Silky Sydney terrier Cherie arrived one morning to complete our 'different' status. Our cornflower blue Vauxhall chugging up and down the town's narrow roads, driven by my mother in a dress with her short hair flying at the wheel soon became a talk of the town. Most of my neighbours were addressed by us children as *maasi,* mother's sister in Gujarati, out of respect. My mother was awarded the English title of 'Aunty'. Soon she was 'Aunty' to everyone who knew her, irrespective of their age, gender, or genealogy.

The most amusing paradox of our lives then was that to the Parsis we were Hindus and to the Hindus we were Parsis. Even today, I still face that discrimination from both sides. Apparently neither side wants us to belong. When I carried idols of Lord Krishna and set up a little toy temple in our room, Mother was only amused. When I copied out Lord Rama's beloved name in my school notebook 1,000 times over, I did not have to hide it. I don't think either of my parents took the practice of religion seriously. They were more spiritual by nature.

For my scientist father, never the conscious believer, it was spiritual guidance you heard with your heart. He would sometimes count grains of wheat while muttering the name of a yet-to-be-named god to help him concentrate on a problem. For Mother, it was an eclectic mix of everything. Even as a child Mother had been against the worship of stone idols or painted images. As a teenager she had set up a small temple in the grounds of her country home in Panchgani and as people lined up for a look, she demonstrated how foolish and ignorant people were to believe that divinity lived in an 'ordinary rock'. As a young woman, long before she had married her previous husband or my dad she had taken an interest in the *Bahai* faith, Sufi theology and yogic ways of life.

I don't think Mother had planned to initiate us into the Zoroastrian faith when she married my father. She was a woman of her time, multi-faceted, hoping to raise her children in multiple faiths. As a child, she had been sent to a Parsi school and had hated the regimental indoctrination there. After that, she was sent to a convent where the German nuns introduced her to stories from the Bible. Personally, she had placed all her trust in the Franciscan Saint Anthony of Padua. As children, therefore, we did not call out to '*Dadarji*', the Prophet Zoroastra like a lot of Parsi children do. We called out to Saint Anthony.

With our Hindu neighbours and all their thirty-six crore gods and goddesses to choose from, Saint Anthony watching over every move (and helped us find lost homework), the world was not such a dangerous place. We did not even know that there were some temples out there where people like us, children of a mixed heritage, were not welcome. We could have gone on like that all our lives, unhindered by hatred, unfettered by form, and unchallenged by custom. Except that after that brief meeting with my grandmother Tehmina and her question about whether we were being taught the Zoroastrian prayers, my father (the non-Parsi) took a giant step towards our religious instruction.

The reason for why my father wanted us to be initiated into the Zoroastrian faith was the same reason for which the Parsis were trying to keep us out – money. Money was important to the Parsis. Some favourite Parsi names are synonymous with wealth, rare metals, and gemstones. *Dhun* (wealth), *Ruby* (ruby), *Manek* (emerald), *Hira* (diamond), *Soonu* (gold), *Cemeen* (silver), *Feroze/Feroza* (turquoise). Need one say more? Father was convinced that our grandmother would mellow if we were brought up Zoroastrian. And so began our deliberate and studied initiation.

Fortunately for us, both our parents and our *dasturji* were able to separate the religion from the practice. With a Parsi mother not completely convinced, a father who had no doubt and several many Hindu neighbours who showered us with stories and *kathas* from their own stash of wisdom, we flitted between the twilight zones of faiths. It was as if there was a threshold of religious instruction that you could step out into or lock yourself in at will. Only, it was someone else's will most of the time and not your own. It was as if this threshold held a door, one side of which was painted a pristine white (like all the doors we had seen in the few Parsi homes we had visited) and the other side was a heavy wooden door bearing metal rings and brass knockers (just like the ones in traditional Hindu homes). Both doors led us inadvertently into a confused and schizophrenic existence.

IV

The OutMarried's Children

'How did your parents meet?'

Who were we? Why were we trying to get into a community that did not want us to belong? Whenever my parents argued about the futility of the initiation (my mother being convinced that nothing would sweeten my grandmother's temper and my father convinced that that was the only thing that would), Mother would recall how she had been insulted at the ancestral *agiary* in the village where she had spent her childhood and told never to darken its door again, and Father would say she had not had the right approach to the whole 'cast off' syndrome the right approach invariably being the offer of a handsome donation to the temple. Our Zoroastrian lessons continued. And so did the merciless teasing at school. I soon got used to the suffix 'half-caste', *adhaa bawa*, *baawi*, and 'half-breed' attached to my name.

With three children at school, a dog and our tortoise Anand, there was enough going on in the house anyway, but it was not long before Mother allowed herself to let her leadership qualities get the better of her. The first thing she did was give the colony a name. We called ourselves the officers' colony (we were all families of government officers, a status to be proud of in those days); we even had an officers' colony club going in an unused car shed. Everything happened through the club. We had annual plays (directed by Mother) and spoofs on Hindi cinema (under Mother's direction). Through Dad's office, Mother managed to get documentaries and promotional feature films. We watched our hero Dev Anand in a full length feature film called *Ek ke baad ek* seated on cotton mats, mattresses, and fossilised cement bags in our colony. The film was about family planning, a buzz phrase of our time.

We went for the annual colony picnic to the riverside (pronounced safe for the children because there was hardly any water in drought-prone Gujarat), and we had mothers showcasing their talent at the annual *garba* festival where the boys were allowed to join in only at the end of the night for the *raas*. This was the dance involving a complex step and jump with lacquered sticks recalling Lord Krishna and his jaunt with the milkmaids. Mother introduced fancy dress parties, magic shows, folk dances, skits, and solo performances (even a ham-handed ballet) to both performers and audiences that had never seen such forms of entertainment before. To her credit, my friend Nina can still dance to *mohey panghat pey nandlal ched gayo rey* from the epic film *Mughal e Azam* at the mature age of sixty-eight.

Fancy dress party with me dressed as a cake

With so much going on, I also had to deal with the business of growing up. Finding solace in the friendship of school friends who were either devoid of prejudice or from 'our side of the country' (Poona) became for me a consciously cultivated habit. Completely unaware of the inheritance that was our due, we grew up looking at career options that would enable us to survive in the world. I remember the day I shared my inner most secret with my school friend Medha Thakar, also originally from Poona.

We were in the grassy lawn of her house and I had written my first essay out of school. I showed it to her and whispered, 'I want to be a writer when I grow up.' She mentioned it to her father who mentioned it to my father, who flew into a rage at such a faulty future plan. It was the age of 'my daughter a doctor, my son an engineer' and writers were 'journalists with *jholas* (literally a cotton handbag slung over your shoulder but also an acronym for a begging bowl) who went hungry. '*Bhookhey marsey*', my father's words went, 'you will starve,' Dad thundered. 'You'll end up walking around the town in torn rubber slippers with an old cotton sling bag over one shoulder, begging for work from newspaper to newspaper.' I tried to think of myself as a doctor but couldn't. Education and career were important.

Father, of course, knew everything about going hungry. 'I am a self-made man,' he would boast. 'Someday, I shall tell you my whole life's story,' he would say. Sadly, he never got around to it, but from what little he did tell us, I could piece together his personal history. Born in a tradition-bound middle class Hindu family in Gujarat, my father lost his mother at the young age of five. The youngest of three siblings, he was brought up by two widowed aunts. As a child, he said, 'There were hardly any nice things to eat in the house. Only widows' foods.' I am assuming that he meant a *sattvik* diet that was free of onions, garlic, and spices as these foods were supposed to arouse the passions, and widows were forbidden from eating them.

Brought up on a dull diet of soupy *dhal* with the sound of the scraping of the bottom of cooking pans accompanying every meal and no demonstrations of affection from his aunts, my father began to look elsewhere for food and comfort. His Dastur School friends, Muslim and Parsi, would often take him home for meals, and my father developed a taste for meat. By the time he was eleven, he had taken a major life-altering decision. Without any papers that connected him to his lineage, he left his father's home, shed his own cultural skin, and offered himself for adoption into a Parsi home.

We only heard this story of his life when one Sunday, in a rare gesture of showing us children a link to his past, Father bundled us into our shining new Ambassador car and took us into the narrow by lanes of Surat in Gujarat. 'I want to show someone the new car,' he said with a rare burst of excitement. I still remember the face of the lady, her head covered in a floral scarf, thrilled to pieces at being introduced to 'the children, the wife and the new car'. I must have been about fourteen. In a sassy teen voice, I asked him if this lady was 'an old flame'. He grinned and said, 'More than that! This is the lady who looked after me when I ran away from home. She gave me work and food. When she saw that I wanted to study, she sent me to school. It is due to her that I have had a decent education.'

Apparently, when the family priest visited the house to teach the Parsi children their prayers, my father would also join in. The old lady laughingly told us that he would get so good at the Zend Avesta teachings that he was soon coaching her children on memorizing parts from the sacred book. That was the day I saw my father for what he was: a runaway child, a self-made man, a survivor. Ironically, we were never taken to visit her again. I think it was enough for the two of them to see that the protégée had done well.

'How did your parents meet?' is a question I am often asked. In an environment where Parsis hardly ever mixed socially with non-Parsis, where great-grandmother would have sacred water sprinkled over the fruit and vegetable basket before it was taken into the house, where all the staff members, painters, masons, and carpenters who worked on the family house 'had to be' Parsi, it is an interesting question. The answer is equally interesting. Having had an English education at the Dastur School at first and then later at the Mission School, my father acquired a British colonial air about him. He learnt how to ride a horse, wear a hat, boots, and breeches, and would often be seen riding into the outskirts of the city. Don't ask me how a homeless lad acquired such expensive tastes and such airs. I really do not know. He never once mentioned any sponsor or patron.

Well, the story goes that my father was out riding a horse one morning when he went past a few fields, some mango groves, and came upon this group of people at a large open well. A calf had fallen into the well and nobody knew how to get the poor animal out. My grandfather happened to be there on one of his rare visits home from Aden. Both Grandfather and Father were mechanically minded. Grandfather had, in fact, installed running water in the family house, a feature unheard of in those days. Water could be pumped up from the well into an overhead tank and then supplied through the house in pipes. Both Grandfather and Father unhitched the pump, used the motor to attach a pulley, made a sling, and pulled the calf out of the well. My father, now a hero, was introduced to the family where he was applauded for being intelligent.

Dad relaxes in his favourite armchair

Mother recalls how Father became a frequent visitor to the house after that. I don't imagine anything romantic transpired between them at first. Mother, in fact, at moments when the food on our table became a bone of contention between them (which was often in the later years of their tumultuous marriage) would recall how her first recollection of my father was that 'he was always hungry'. This may have been true because even after he got the debilitating Alzheimer's disease, my father never forgot his love for good food and would ask me if there were 'five things to eat'. Interestingly, the other thing he never forgot was anyone showing any kind of 'insubordination', a word he used his whole life through. Hardly able to walk himself, unable to articulate his thoughts or his needs, he would waggle a finger angrily if he ever found any of our staff members seated on a chair in his presence. When he walked past, they were to stand at attention. Even as a younger man in a government office, his exaggerated sense of self-exaltation was legendary. He had been known to have thrown a shoe at someone for 'insubordination'.

Bringing him into the family fold after the heroic rescue of the drowning calf was one thing, but I don't think the family expected my mother to fall in love with him with the intention to marry. She must have expected some flak from her own parents. She may have had the plunk to live 'outside' the community, but I do not think she anticipated such venom and hatred from the other close relatives. Her father was the youngest of nine siblings (seven brothers and two sisters), all of who had either close business or filial ties.

The eldest brother Pirojsha controlled some of my grandfather's finances after he returned from Aden to India, and Mother had to visit him on occasions. After she married my father, however, things changed. He did settle her dues, but his wife, my mother's aunt Goolbai, would not allow her to step through the door. All their business transactions were carried outside, Mother says, with her uncle carrying on a conversation with her from within the house while she stood at the door. After every such visit, Mother would come back distressed and upset. Eldest uncle never once asked her in. He never enquired after the children. Perhaps, according to him, we were illegitimate or invisible.

'Someday these things will change,' my father would say by way of comforting my mother. And one day, they did. Eldest Uncle's only granddaughter announced to her horrified parents and grandparents that she was planning to marry a Hindu from Kashmir. I have no idea of what transpired between the granddaughter, but for us it was a windfall. We were summoned to Eldest Uncle's house. Mother and Father were dressed in their best, and we girls were put in fluffy white dresses with pink bows and our brother in a two-piece suit with a maroon bow tie, a dress code for the well-appointed Parsi children of that time. We were taken, for the first time, to meet Eldest Uncle and his wife and their Parsi nurse who was by then an integral part of the family. We were given a syrupy rose drink and cookies at the table and a chocolate wrapped in gold foil that had come all the way from England. Eldest Uncle's wife continued to refer to her Hindu grandson-in-law as her granddaughter's lover and not her husband.

The atonement (if at all it can be called that) had come a tad too late, however. Eldest Uncle was too way past his prime to set any new trends. Mother's first cousins were far too many and too spread out geographically to have been influenced by this homecoming. I did not meet any of my second cousins until well into my adulthood (my siblings hardly know them even today) and one of my biggest sore points is that bigotry and prejudice got in the way of our getting to know one another as children.

Funnily enough, this deep-seated prejudice against us did not stop one of my second cousins from spending weekends with us in our little house in officers' colony. Away from home and at engineering college, where the hostel offered only vegetarian meals, Sam would come over on weekends, enjoy meat-rich meals at our table, and ask for my non-Parsi father's assistance over a niggling legal matter concerning the family-owned *agiary* in some remote corner of Gujarat. My father used his own network to take him to officials in the charity commissioner's office to find a way out of the legal tangle and ensure that he got the trusteeship of the *agiary*.

Truth be told, he never failed to continue to visit my father till he passed away, always addressing him as 'Uncle' – this despite the fact that he had branded us as 'non-Parsis'.

Father never saw the hypocrisy or irony in this, but I did. The *agiary* trusteeship claim had begged a question. The original trust deed, however misguided this may sound, only allowed a male heir to succeed. Sam wanted it, although he had descended from his mother. I do not know how they worked around this but they did. It was clear that when Sam wanted it, he could set aside the gender issue, but when it came to us being accepted, he pulled out the gender card branding us as unacceptable. What manner of *manasni gavasni kunasni*, 'good thought, good words, good deeds', was this? Where was the *righteousness* so preached in the beloved Avesta? When he is confronted today about what counts in my register as a double-standards, his defence is that we were 'cousins, yes, but not Parsis'.

Mother's most vivid recollection of her aunts was a blurry image of them diving into their prayer books as soon as she paid them a visit. Some of her first cousins would look at her 'as if she was a bug under a microscope'. It was as if she had become something of a curiosity just because she had chosen to marry 'outside'. We were never invited to weddings, *navjotes*, or any other family outings. Unknown to us, however, *their* children were growing up in England and other parts of India and harboured no such prejudice.

The story of how I met my cousin Ardeshir for the first time is amazing. A rather curious pair walked into our Bandra house one morning. A middling gentleman (Ardeshir) and an Arab come up the stairs, one holding his cap and the other his prayer beads. 'I am your cousin's son Adi,' said the gentleman, 'and this is the grandson of the Arab servant your father had in Aden. This man has something to say to you.' Mother was surprised but tried not to show it. *What the grandson of an Arab servant could have to say to us here in India*, we wondered. Besides, none of us knew any Arabic.

Through sign language and a smattering of the few Arabic words between Mother and Adi, we heard what the Arab had to say. Pieced together, he was actually saying that his grandfather had been handed the keys to the shop that my grandfather Rustomjee owned when he left Aden for India. His Arab grandfather had looked after the shop in the hope that the original owner would return. He began to run the shop exactly the way Grandfather would have run it. The Little Aden Provision Store did well. The shop had since been passed on to his son and now to his grandson. He had come all this way to pay Mother what he thought he owed. 'God will not grant me a place in Paradise if the matter is not settled,' he said. And so, through the few Indians that still remained in Aden, he had managed to contact Adi and had travelled all this way. True to character Adi had rushed him over to Mother.

One would think Mother would be grateful for this windfall. This offer of payment for a shop that remained all but a memory had come completely out of the blue. Anybody else would have taken whatever was offered and given the man a cup of tea. Not Mother. Although she had been a school teacher all her life, her 'business genes' bubbled up to the surface. She began to wonder what the shop was worth when Grandfather Rustomjee had left Aden. She began to add numbers to the years that had gone past and came up with a considerable figure. Naturally, the Arab was surprised. However, businessmen and women have their own language, and when business was done, I am certain I saw the Arab smiling. Mother, on the other hand, went laughing all the way to the bank.

For me, however, this meeting opened up a new kind of treasure. I suddenly had cousins. I was fascinated by their personal histories, their choice of profession, and their interpersonal relationships. What's more, as a late entrant, I could see a pattern that they said that they had never noticed. In every group of siblings, I noticed that there ran a common thread, and this was that no one sibling resembled the other. This included the three of us as well. There is absolutely no physical resemblance between us. It's the same with all the branches in the family. Of course, some of my cousins insist that their brothers looked alike as children but now I do not see any resemblance. There is nothing in their height, body shape, or facial characteristic that is remotely alike. I find that fascinating and curious.

Equally curious is the fact that a lot of us are, in some way or another, connected with architecture, publishing, and printing. I write on Goan architecture and have published some of my own books. My cousin Gool works for a printing press in Mumbai. Her brother Dimpy is a practising architect. Our cousin Shirin was in publishing and worked for magazines. Our cousin Ardeshir is a qualified architect. He also writes. What is it that makes us veer towards these professions? Is it something in our genes or just plain coincidence? As far as I know, none of our fathers, mothers, or grandparents were remotely interested in these professions. Yes, Mother did her best to inculcate an interest in music, painting, and embroidery in me, but I only made brief and uninterested attempts at learning these arts just to please her. She would have liked to see me as a professional dancer in Bharata Natyam, but I only went as far as doing the peacock dance to the tortured groans of my fellow students at the school annual day.

Mother would sit with the harmonium and teach me to play the basic notes while she sang. My music lessons did not graduate beyond that. Mother had also found me a mandolin teacher to tutor me in the school holidays, but I was hopeless at it. To my good fortune, there was never enough money in the house to invest in any more musical instruments. My drawing teacher at school cringed every time he had a look at my drawing book. My needlework teacher was compelled to gnash her teeth at my crotchet. My interest in learning music, painting, or dance was eclipsed when I got to my teens, and my giddy head began to be filled with other interests. To my mother and my art teachers at school, I was a disappointment.

Mother had always been the student who walked away with all the prizes at school. Most of the books in her library had come as prizes she had won at various grades in school. She had done her Senior Cambridge from St. Joseph's Convent in Panchgani where the exam papers were set in England and standards were so high that the examination board had done away with ranking completely. Being the only daughter of 'well-to-do' parents, there was no question of her leaving home to join a college. She understood this quite early on and decided to make up for it by reading. She read voraciously and was mostly 'self-taught' in every subject except science.

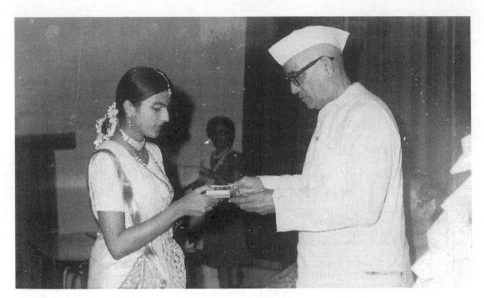

I get a medal in Good Conduct at school

When I was ready to leave school at the Convent of Jesus and Mary in Baroda, I had not won a single prize. Mother could not bear the thought of her eldest daughter leaving school without a single award, book prize, or medal. She began working on Sister Aquinas, then our school principal. 'But the list of prize winners has already been handed to me by the teachers,' Sister Aquinas protested. 'Then introduce a new prize, a medal, anything,' Mother demanded. Mother held such a sway over our school principal that she finally relented. A Good Conduct medal was introduced for the first and probably the last time. Much to my embarrassment, Mother spent the next couple of months parading me and the silver medal to any hapless guest who walked in through our door. I have been obliged to be on 'good conduct' behaviour ever since.

Always fascinated with stories, much to my delight, each new cousin came with his or her own bouquet of stories. And as we grew older, the stories that had once been hushed up 'in front of the children' were now being aired and opened out leaf by petal. Take, for instance, the story of Jaijibai, our grandfather's widowed sister. The story goes that once widowed, poor Jaiji was thrown out of her marital home and packed off to her maternal home with her two children Dara and Nergish. Apparently, none of the widow's brothers was keen on taking on the onus of looking after this fatherless family, except for my grandfather, known for his generosity and kind heart. His signature was 'Your left hand should not know of the charity you do with your right hand.' Dara, Nergish, and my mother grew up together as children with seven-year-old Dara playing the role of the 'man of the house' in the absence of grown men.

It was an all-woman household. My great-grandmother ruled the house, supervising everything including the food rations to her widowed daughter and her children. Little has been documented about their sister Ratan, who must have been an independent, creative, and innovative individual, a single woman with a mind of her own. My guess is that Ratanbai was probably raised by her parents to think independently and look after the farms and houses with the view of keeping her at home. Unmarried and unfettered by marital responsibility, she was their insurance against old age. It was not an unusual practice amongst the Parsis of India. In the absence of health insurance, with no guarantee that your sons (in this case, seven) or their wives (more than seven) would take care of you when you grew old, investing in a daughter made sense.

Patell Cottage, the Siganpore House

So there it was this all-woman household with my great-grandmother Goolbai with her two daughters, widowed Jaiji and the unmarried Ratan. Then there was my grandmother Tehmina and her daughter Manijeh or Mani (also called *levti,* mudskipper in jest) and a retinue of female servants, the prime position held by Soonamai, who was apparently devoted to my mother. What is astounding in this day and age is that much contrary to popular belief the stigma of being a widow and living a widow's life of austerity and strict religious orthodoxy was being followed in this Parsi Zoroastrian household, Jaiji was made to observe all the taboos associated with being a widow. She was never taken to weddings or 'happy occasions'. She was never present for any celebrations. The auspicious *chalk na dabba* that doors were stamped with on celebratory occasions were never handed to her.

When guests arrived on auspicious occasions and a vermillion dot was to be placed on their foreheads as a mark of respect and welcome, it was always to be done by the *suhagan,* the married ladies of the house. This would naturally exclude the two daughters, Jaiji and Ratanbai. Gradually, the widowed sister confined herself to the one single small room on the ground floor which she shared with a treasure trove of biscuits, *batasas*, and pickles while the unmarried one plunged into the affairs of the farms and the estate. The children were given a free run of the house and grew up in the company of the servants. At ninety-one, my mother was more comfortable in the company of her ayahs, nurses, and maids and would happily follow their directions over mine. She had obviously gone back to her childhood.

With the servants came a whole bundle of superstitions. 'Never go for a bath after a meal', 'Never talk at the dinner table, the food goes into the stomachs of donkeys', 'Never go to the river bank in the evenings. The *djinns* and spirits cohabit there', and 'If you put your ears close enough to the well, you will hear the fairies that live there.' Visiting dervishes and *sadhus* also made their mark on the children. Unsupervised by the adults in the house, they became part of the crowd of supplicants. They were fortunate to have met with some really evolved people because they soon learnt how to meditate, chant, and even levitate. Raised in a large two-storied mansion surrounded by mango, coconut, wood apple, and tamarind trees, the children did their best to emulate their peers in the village. When they went to the only school in the village, my mother said, they would slip off their shoes, rub mud on their clothes, and mess up neatly braided hairdos so that they would be more comfortable in the company of their lesser-privileged shoeless schoolmates. They too wanted to belong. They too wanted to not be 'non'.

Jaiji remained largely unseen and voiceless in the big household. She was left attending to the most mundane of household chores. In those days, almost everything got delivered to the door. Milk, eggs, fish, and fruit came in large round baskets delivered by men in bullock carts. Besides, there was also the produce from the farm, baskets loaded with mangoes, guavas, and berries. Great-grandmother would make weekly trips to the city in her one horse carriage (for which she would dress in her best Chinese embroidered silk *garas*) for the family's stock of biscuits, cake, and other treats from Surat's famous Dotiwala Bakery.

Everything was purchased in large quantities for reasons of thrift and to save 'horse power'. Most of it went to Jaiji's corner room where it kept company with other large jars packed with pickles and *murabbas* that were made at home. Come February and the air would be filled with the musk of mango blossoms. In April and May, palm-sized fingers of ginger and floors carpeted with raw mangoes and bananas from the farms would be laid out in beds on grass mats with their 'noses turned up like nawabs'.

Very few of these delivery men were ever admitted into the hallowed portals of the main house. They either made their deliveries to the servant's quarters behind the house or set up shop in the back porch. There was, however, an exception to the rule. If the vendor or supplier was a Parsi, he would be taken in and even offered a cup of tea and a little snack from the kitchen. One such vendor was a gentleman, whose first name escapes everybody including Mother despite her elephantine memory. This gentleman, whose last name was Shahuna, would make pickles, jams, jellies, and syrups and bring them over to the house for the family to sample. Jaiji was in the forefront for these domestic purchases. Old man Shahuna soon became acceptable.

V

The Widow Meets a Man

'We were told to stay out of the room when Uncle visited.'

The gentleman took to coming over in the heat of the afternoons when the entire household was asleep. The children, of course, never took a siesta. 'We were told to stay out of the room when Uncle visited,' Mother recalled with a gleam in her eye, 'but we never did. We would look for some excuse to go in.' Considering the strict Victorian morals of those days, nothing much must have happened. 'What if this social interaction had turned into love between the widowed sister and this man? Would they have been encouraged to marry?' is the question.

Orthodoxy and superstition would have probably won in the end. The fact that these two gentle souls had to meet in the middle of the afternoon, the fact that everyone knew what was going on and yet no one took the initiative to give it legitimacy, and the fact that this gentleman almost always brought his little nephew along 'for appearance sake' speaks for its times. I've often wondered what governed their thought processes in those days.

What sort of family had Jaiji married into and what compulsions made the Vanias turn their daughter-in-law away along with her two young children? All we know is that Jaiji was married to one Ardeshir Bejanji Vania from Surat. Going by the patriarchal nature of the society then, was there a tussle to keep one of the two children (the boy of course) for themselves? And, more tragically, why was it such a struggle for this widow (born into a farming family and probably married into a reasonably well-to-do household) to survive the 'widow' status?

My cousin Rati, Jaiji's granddaughter and Dara's daughter, does testify to some interest in the boy child from the Vania family. When Jaiji's son Dara was nearing the age when they finished school in those days, he was brought to Bombay to do his matriculation, an important qualification that would enable him to get a job in the city. I don't think they bothered about Nergish, the girl child or her education. She was left to her own devices in the village of Siganpore, running around barefoot in and out of the village school. Rati thinks it was Dara's uncle (Ardeshir Vania's brother) who brought Dara to Bombay, and later, when Dara landed a job with the Singer Sewing Machine Company, Jaiji was brought to Bombay to be looked after by her 'earning' son. Nergish, of course, was not expected to get either an education or a job, so she just 'lay about' in the big Siganpore house, waiting for marriage.

Nergish and Jal in Hubli

Life, of course, has its own way of getting even. Old Mr Shahuna, this gentleman vendor of pickles and syrups, used to bring his little nephew to give his afternoon visits some legitimacy. The children were put to 'pasture' in the fields and would run around the fields, climb trees, and play with the *ticca gharries*, horse carriages, all afternoon. Between the four of them, Dara, Nergish, Mani, and Jal, they whipped up mayhem. No one quite knows how this childhood friendship turned to love, but Nergish and Jal married each other in a simple Zoroastrian ceremony in Siganpore while still in their teens. I don't know if he was present at the wedding, but Old Uncle Shahuna, wherever he was, must have had a good laugh. Nergish and Jal have a son Kersi who lives in Chennai with his wife Zavera. They have two children and a set of twin grandchildren. None of them, however, know anything of the family history. Ask Kersi a question about the family, and he will hand you his trademark phrase, 'No clue'.

In fact, years later, I had taken it upon myself to call my cousins and other relatives and inform them of a death in the family. I was given a list when Jal Uncle passed away. I had never met Gool Patel but decided to call her anyway. When I called Gool to let her know that Jal Uncle had passed away, her first question to me was 'Who is Jal Uncle and why are you calling me?' When I tried to explain who he was and who I was, she said before slamming the phone down, 'Is this a joke? First of all, I don't know who Jal Uncle is and second of all, I don't know who you are'. I was persistent and called her once again. I was paid for my diligence. Gool is one of my closest and best-loved cousins today.

The turn of phrase 'no clue' just about sums up the rest of the family's ignorance. No one seems to know much about Ratanbai, Jaijibai, or the two children Dara and Nergish. The family tree makes no mention of the female children in the family, so one can hardly expect a mention of the Patell daughters. There are no notes, no poems, and no odes to enterprising daughters as there are to the enterprising sons. What a pity then that some of this gender bias should percolate down to the third generation of men in the family. One of our cousins denies Jaiji's children and grandchildren their right to claim a Patell ancestry. 'How can Jaiji's children and grandchildren claim they are Patells?' he questions. 'Jaiji was a girl.' Some of my cousins refuse to acknowledge that there were two daughters. They just believe there was one, the widow with the two children. You only get remembered if you marry and have children.

In Rati's own words, 'Dara was nine and Nergish was a year old when their father passed away. We never heard our dad Dara speak of our grandfather. There was nothing amiss in that. They just did not talk about these things in those days. When Mehra Aunty was selling the ancestral house in Surat, the *gaam nu gher*, the house in the village where the family history really began, she found one table that belonged to Ardeshir Bejanji Vania and another table with Jai written on it. We did not know how to bring it to our little home in Bombay, so Mani Aunty helped us out. She had it packed and transported, and it was sent to our Sanjan flat and is still in very good shape. Our grandmother Jai had no personal income, despite coming from such a prosperous family, but she brought up her children with great care and austerity. This used to upset my Aunt Nergish, but my dad Dara would say, "If we throw rose petals at others, then we get the fragrance. We scatter thorns they will only turn around and prick us."

'"The others are growing up in the lap of luxury while we children are living in penury," Nergish would complain. "Luxury is artificial poverty. Contentment is natural wealth," he would comfort her. The six pillars for living a good life, according to him, were contentment, love, truth, dignity, happiness, and faith.'

Dara was truly a wonderful man. Having perhaps suffered as a child, he had insisted that his own daughters should educate themselves and make their lives meaningful. Rati would often ask her father if he did not miss having a son, and he would say, 'Not at all! God has given me three daughters who are like three sons!' Then he would tease by saying, 'Only thing is, when God was distributing brains, my daughters ran to God with baskets so all the brains slipped away!' That could not have been true because my cousin Rati Wadia worked as a teacher all her life and retired as principal of Queen Mary's School. Having seen the gender bias and the prejudices in his own grandmother's home, Dara was completely sympathetic when my mother married a 'non', a *parjaat*, an outsider. He never treated us as 'half-castes'. He visited us often, and he and his wife Freny had us over in their Shapur Baug home whenever we came to Bombay from Baroda on vacation.

Both Rati and Pervez think their father Dara had been brought to Bombay from Siganpore by their uncle (their father's brother) Merwanji and his wife Lily to live in the congested residential neighbourhood of Khetwadi. At some point, the children realised that they had three uncles who had offered to look after them. All we know is that Nergish was also brought to Bombay later and sent to the Tutorial School, a Parsi institution owned by the Banaji family. They lived in Khetwadi, a congested area of Bombay, opposite a well-appointed mansion named Commissariat House. The Commissariat family had, in Jane Austen-style, four daughters, and each one of them was less than a year apart. Romance developed between three out of four of the Commissariat sisters and three boys from across the road, and they all ended up marrying 'across front doors'.

VI

Dara Starts a Family

'Bombay then was one of the safest places on earth.'

Dara married Freny, got himself a job in the Singer Sewing Company at first, and then at Unilever as a salesman from where he retired thirty-two years later as a sales supervisor. Well-read, self-tutored, and refined in his mannerisms, Dara had looks that were often compared with Clark Gable or David Niven, Hollywood heroes of the time. Dara also had the gift of the gab and was fluent in both Gujarati and English, talent that stood him in good stead at work. Both Dara and Freny had passed their matriculation, but in those days, the qualification was of such a high standard that they were like graduates of today. 'You can choose your friends but you cannot choose your relatives,' Dara would say, but when Nergish and Jal married and had a little son that old saying was put to the test. Kersi loved his *mamu*, his uncle Dara, and was loath to part with him except for school. Both families were close with Rati and Kersi being initiated into the Zoroastrian faith on the same day together, like siblings. They were more than cousins; they were inseparable as children.

What Dara and Freny lost out on a higher education, they made up with their reading, drawing inspiration from books, and meeting people who were spiritually inclined. Like most parents of the time, both Dara and Freny set a great score by prizes won at school. Freny had received a prize titled *1001 Poems* and that was one of her most treasured possessions long after she had finished school. She would read poems from the book to her girls often and some of those quotes have remained with Rati, Pervez, and Hira till today. Dara had named his middle daughter after his *maasi*, his aunt Ratanbai, as a tribute to her fiery spirit.

Dara also had a corner in the house where he used to read his favourite Agatha Christie novels. The girls grew up with a love for books. 'I feel like a king today because of the legacy they left us,' Rati says. When Dara and Freny married, they decided to live on their own, away from the uncles. Houses in the Bombay Central area were affordable and ideal to begin life together. Pervez, their first daughter was born at Dalal Estate in their new home. It was a Parsi enclave but not a *baug* run by a family trust. Flats and houses were privately owned, and one could buy, sell, or rent at will.

'Whether it was foresight or there was trouble brewing, I do not know. Bombay then was one of the safest places on earth,' says Rati. 'Even so, my dad decided to move his young family to the newly built Shapurji Broacha Baug (run by the Bai Bhikaji H. Bennet Trust) the first Parsi colony that had a lift and tiled floors.' They were begging for people to come there to stay, and Dara was keen on living amongst 'his own' there. Shapur Baug must have been so attractive then. There was cross ventilation, a rare architectural feature, and no two front doors faced each other. All the flats were lovely and breezy, something most Bombayites were fascinated with. The move to Shapur Baug proved to be the right decision because years later, there was a communal riot in the Muslim-dominated Bombay Central station area, and rioters had set Dalal Estate on fire. I remember the Godrej cupboard melted to nothing just like an ice cream cone in the heat. One couple burned to death because the wife refused to leave her invalid husband behind in the flat. It is a tragic story that has gone largely undocumented.

'My daddy Dara chose this flat because there was a doctor next door, and he thought having a medical man as a neighbour would be a great advantage. He also looked at the flat and thought it would a healthy alternative to the Bombay Central place because it was so airy. For someone to consider a rental for its cross ventilation and to attribute good health to an airy open environment was itself extraordinary in those days.'

Meeting up with cousins and making them your inner circle of friends seems to be the most natural thing in the world. Befriending people is never easy under the best of circumstances, but when I first came to Mumbai in 1981, I was introduced to a fascinating social concept, unique to the city and totally new to me personally. When I took a local train from Bandra to Churchgate every morning, I would meet up with a girl named Serena. We would take the same train every morning, sit by my side and chat all the way to Churchgate. I never once asked her where she lived, where she worked, what her last name was, or anything about her family. She was my 'train friend'. We mostly talked about trains. We never once met outside of the local train, and it never occurred to either of us to take this friendship beyond the limits of the train journey. So it was with 'park' friends, people you walked with in the park, and 'bus' friends, people you only met on the BEST bus.

The only other cousin I became friends with in the 1980s was Mahrukh. Most of my mother's aunts and uncles had shunned her when she married my father. With seven uncles and two aunts, their wives, husbands, and children, we should have been a close-knit clan but because of Mother having married 'outside', no one wanted to know us. Jaiji, the widowed aunt's children, Dara and Nergish, and their children, Pervez, Rati, Hira, and Kersi, were the exception. On my grandmother's side, there were three cousins who were also unaffected by the 'outmarriage'. Kamal Aunty and Bejan Uncle in Nagpur were unmoved by Mother's marriage. Their children Arnavaz, Mahrukh, Tinaaz, and Shiraz, two of which were to marry 'outside' themselves, were our only relatives. Kamal Aunty and Bejan Uncle would often visit us in Panchgani, forever subjecting us to taste their mulberry jams and strawberry soufflés.

VII

The House in Panchgani

'Study hard and get good jobs, then you can hire a cook. I don't want my daughters to spend the rest of their lives cooking and making rotis.'

Unlike my siblings who were encouraged to brave the outside world, I was the one tied to my mother's apron strings. Father was the one who had done all the tying. When I was learning how to ride a bicycle, both Mother and Father were very proud of me. Until the moment when I crashed into our neighbour's car head-on, fell off the cycle, and was up on the seat again, scared but unscathed. Dad heard about the collision and put a stop to my cycling lessons. 'Don't worry about the cycle,' he said, 'I'll just teach you how to drive a car.' So before I turned a 'full' fifteen, my father had put me behind the wheels of our 1956 cornflower-blue Vauxhall with the key words of 'coordination' and 'eyes on the road'. By the time I was sixteen, I was driving myself to school with Dad sitting beside me an indulgent passenger, giving every traffic policemen we were whizzing past the royal wave.

It was the same wave that dismissed me from entering the kitchen in our two-bedroom government colony home. 'Study hard and get good jobs, then you can hire a cook. I don't want my daughters to spend the rest of their lives cooking and making *rotis*.' The office peon Magan who also doubled up as our cook would defy this dictate. When Dad was at work, he would beckon us with a wagging finger and a wink and teach us how to make chapattis. The secret lessons helped. The pressure of getting caught at chapatti-making resulted in my being able to roll them out at breakneck speed so that I could roast two at a time on both gas burners. I was proud of my chapatti-making skills and would run to the neighbours to show off. But on 'certain days of the month', even they would not allow me to touch the stove. How could I be considered unclean? I had, after all, now graduated to tucking a gauze pad, hung like a hammock, on two beaded thongs between my legs.

In those days, the colony had a tradition of giving the first chapatti of the day to the crow, the second to the cow, and then keeping the rest for the household. Both the crow and the cow knew where to go for lunch. I still remember the gentle face of the brown cow that came to the kitchen window for the first chapatti of the day. As for the crow, he would eat out of Mother's hand. Soon a three-banded chipmunk joined us for early lunch, and we named her Chiki, after the demanding raucous 'chik chik chik' she would take up when she was really hungry. Mother carried on with the 'family tradition' of feeding the crows wherever we moved. Years later, when we set up home in Mumbai, she would send for a loaf of sliced bread for the crows. Even today when 'our' crows spot a melon in the fruit basket, they start a caucus until they are given a sliver of the sliced shell.

My chapatti-making skills were improving. I had enough time to think. What was I being groomed for really? A career woman or a spinster who would look after her parents when they grew old? I was also told almost every single day to 'watch out for the little ones' and that it was a solemn duty of the older siblings to look after the younger ones. Dad was a scientist by training and Mother a teacher by accident. Mother had had no formal education past her Senior Cambridge from St Joseph's in small-town Panchgani. Dad had, on the other hand, a college degree from the Wadia College in Pune followed by a PhD from Texas University, Austin, Texas. She was the painter, the poet, the singer, and the crucible of family values and refinement. He was always the one to say, 'Be practical.' It was heart breaking to see him snub her for her poor education and non-scientific bend of mind. He would encourage us to laugh at her for her inability to grasp 'simple scientific principles'. He fell from grace the day I learnt that it had been her money that had sent him to the United States for his PhD in the first place.

Mother had mortgaged her house in Panchgani to send Dad to the United States. Dad's uncle had loaned them the money with the property as collateral. They were in debt to Dad's maternal uncle much before they were even married. Her faith in Dad's ability to pay it back must have been steadfast. It took us years to understand why 'Ballu *Mama*' would come from Surat and park himself on a chair in the verandah for hours. As children, we used to refer to him as Good Luck Uncle because he would always come with a bag of Good Luck washing soap chips. Mother and Dad were in his debt, and yet he was gracious enough to bring a bag of the soap chips that he used to make in his detergent factory. If they had not been able to pay off this debt, we would never have had the Panchgani house.

In Goa, a family deity is treated like just another member of the family. 'Has he eaten? Has he been dressed? Has he left for his immersion?' For us, it has been the houses. They've been like hard-working members of a family that have given of themselves and asked for very little in return. Buying the Panchgani house, Abbas Villa, in Mother's name, when she was a little over nineteen years old was a stroke of genius. Grandfather Rustomjee may or may not have had foresight. I don't think they bought houses in those days as an investment like we do today. The story of Abbas Villa and how we acquired it needs to be told.

Abbas Villa in Panchgani

Panchgani was a colonial hill station in the late 1800s founded by two British brothers, John and James Chesson. Poladpur, at the foot of the hills that take you up to Mahableshwar from the Mahad flats in the Konkan, was a town known for its iron ore deposits. However, the early British surveyors realised the potential of these hills as recreation areas beneficial for the health of the British in Bombay, and instead of turning these hills into mining areas, they recommended them as summer resorts. Consumption, cholera, and plague were threatening the lives of many Englishmen, women, and children in Bombay and the government was on the lookout for a safer and healthier place to sojourn and educate their young. While Mahableshwar, eighteen kilometres away, was considered good enough for the Governor of Bombay and his entire retinue as a summer escape, Panchgani was selected as a place where one could build good schools, sanatoriums, and a hospital.

Weather wise, this made perfect sense. Panchgani was an all-weather place, where one could stay in comfort even during the rains. Mahableshwar, on the other hand, had to be emptied completely every year, its fine houses boarded up with grass screens as protection against the cold and harsh monsoon winds. The British from Bombay put up schools and a hospital in Panchgani. I doubt if there was an existing village there before this British settlement. It is clearly a British town, now run by its own 150-year-old municipality. Local stone was used for the construction of schools, houses, and hospitals, the railings, the glassware, and the furniture were direct imports from Poona and Bombay. In fact, furniture was often carted back and forth every season when the British residents of Panchgani and Mahableshwar moved themselves in and out, 'lock, stock, and barrel'.

Taking a completely virgin area covered in indigenous trees and inhabited by wildlife and converting it into a place for human habitation must not have been easy. Like they did in other parts of India (in the tea and coffee plantations in Munnar, Kerala, for example) the government coaxed pioneering British planters to tame wild lands. Forest species were replaced by the tall silver oaks imported from the south of India and several slopes going down to the river Krishna were covered in coffee. Although Panchgani began to be known as a hill station, I think this description was applied to the town much after the British left India. Panchgani was the town established for education and convalescence. Mahableshwar was the hill station, with its Governor's summer palace, its clubs, and its spacious bungalows constructed on high plinths.

Panchgani, on the other hand, was the 'low plinth hill station'. Unlike Mahableshwar, Panchgani did not have the airs of high society. There were no clubs, balls, parties, picnics, race courses, or 'rides' taken by the 'lords and ladies' of British Indian society. If there were horses in Panchgani, they were owned privately and kept in private stables attached to the new bungalows. There were horses that residents used to ride from one peak to another and not just for the joy. In fact, around and about the year 1889, there was a desperate call from the then Government of Bombay to the residents of Bombay to come to Panchgani and set up summer homes. As an incentive, these pioneers were offered ninety-nine-year leases on lands that they would occupy on nominal rents and on which they could build their homes, raise their families, and provide livelihoods to the several butchers, bakers, barbers, cobblers, saddlers, and fruit and vegetable vendors. People were actually given incentives to come settle in Panchgani.

Like in all the other British hill stations and campsites, the town grew mainly in service of the British who came to occupy and live there. Boots and saddles that the British needed were made by the cobblers; tailors mended and sewed British-style suits and dresses. Barbers set up shops in the bazaar where they shaved their male patrons and gave them haircuts. Dhobis took laundry down to Wai and carried on with their washing in the Krishna River. In fact, there is a whole lane named Dhobi Gully where second- and third-generation laundrymen work and live even today. Bakers baked bread, buns, and Anglo-Indian favourites like cream rolls, fan biscuits, and *burun pão*, light and crusty round bread loaves, the English adaptation of the Portuguese *unde* for the British breakfast table.

Chick peas were sold in the town initially for the horses, and once roasted on hot sand beds became popular with residents as well. British garden lovers brought with them strawberry plants, iceberg lettuce, purple cabbage, and dog roses, and filled Panchgani gardens with roses, petunias, pansies, morning glory, and thunder lilies. Honey was collected from the trees in the forests and brought to the weekly market as were greens. This fitted in perfectly with the Indian weekly market system. Even today, every village and town has a weekly market with complete coordination of the weekly calendar between towns. The many honey, jam, and *chikki* shops in the Panchgani bazaar are simply second- or third-generation offshoots of these original artisans. *Dhangars*, tribal herders, brought in their herds of goat and sheep to graze on the slopes of Panchgani and, then finding conditions favourable, stayed on, converted to Islam, and brought in their own mixed heritage.

Soon the Parsi, Bohri, and Hindu merchants from Bombay considered it fashionable to send their own children to the schools in Panchgani. While the British parents sent their girls to St Joseph's Convent (Catholic) up on Tableland Road or to Kimmins (Protestant), and boys went to St Peter's (also Protestant) on Mahableshwar Road. Almost every student in the 1880s was a boarder with schools divided on religious and caste lines. In fact, most schools did not have secular names until 1947 when the British left India and independent India donned the garb of being secular to regain its respect from the Western world. Before that, however, Batha High School was called the Parsi School; Anjuman-e-Islam, the Muslim School; Sanjeevan Vidyalaya was the Hindu School; and so on. One can safely assume that parents sent their children to the schools where religious instruction was included.

The table mountain or Tableland, actually a series of five small plateaus, was used for walks and later for football matches. It was treated for all practical purposes as an open ground. Panch 'giri' or five mountains may have got corrupted over usage to Panch 'gani' giving the new town its name in the local Marathi. For the pleasure of watching the sunset and enjoying their sundowners, Parsi residents of Panchgani were seen at what began to be called Parsi Point overlooking the Krishna. Sydney Point was named after a government surveyor who surveyed the first lands; Harrison's Folly named after a stubborn British resident who refused to kowtow to the fierce monsoon winds and repeatedly built his house on the ridge overlooking Wai and the Krishna valley.

Like they had done in all towns in British India, the local government had a well-defined bazaar area where the artisans and traders could be found, the weekly market held, and the local festivals celebrated. The bungalows and cottages were scattered in winding lanes around the town centre, and life for most locals revolved around the bazaar. For those who had not yet acquired lands or built bungalows, there were a few hotels. With a few exceptions, these hotels were open only to European guests. Prospect Hotel, our nearest neighbour, had a sign saying, 'FOR EUROPEANS ONLY'. As most guests arrived in carriages, they were referred to as 'passengers'. Hundred and twenty-five years down the road, our maid Chingubai, still refers to our guests as 'passengers'.

All Panchgani residents, without exception, are immigrants from other towns and villages that were first brought in by the demands of a British lifestyle in the hills. So where does the xenophobic posturing come from? Ironically, when there is a class issue or a land dispute, someone will try and play the 'you versus them' card. They will try to create a rift on the grounds that you are an outsider, that they are *Panchgani chey maanse*, the sons of the soil. To counter this move, I have often asked the ubiquitous Indian question of all time: 'Where are you from?' And the sheepish response will invariably be the name of a village *near* about Panchgani, Wai, Satara, or Mahableshwar.

Strangely enough, the eastern half of Panchgani, all its hills and valleys included, was given to the early British residents as 'freehold' lands. The western half was given as 'leasehold'. This meant that the whole town was divided into 'freehold' and 'leasehold'. Freehold lands were lands that could be purchased and sold at will by land owners. For residents who were unable to pay for the lands outright and become fully fledged owners, there was the option of leasing or renting the lands from the government. To give the lease holders a feeling of being stakeholders in the development of the new town, these leases were given for ninety-nine years, considered to span two generations at the time.

It was in this fledgling town that Henry Couldrey arrived in Panchgani. Did he stay at the Prospect Hotel while he was working the hills, prospecting for iron ore in Poladpur and the hills between Wai and Panchgani? Unsuccessful in his mission, did he then decide to stay on, take the lands on lease, and do something else instead? Did he have a family that he thought might someday enjoy the ninety-nine-year-old lease? I know very little about him except that he leased the lands on which stand the Dhun Heta Bungalow, Jena Cottage, and Joy Cottage today. He leased these lands for ninety-nine years in the year 1889. He must have gardeners and grooms to look after his horses, for he had a full stable with five doors that opened out into the garden.

For someone who may have not made a fortune in iron ore, Henry Couldrey must have been a man of means. He was also a man who exercised caution because he built a small cottage at first at the top of the road that he named Rose Villa. Couldrey lived there at first, close to the road from where he could probably ride or walk up to Tableland. The rest of the land was untamed jungle then, and a tigress and her cubs lived in a cave above the land. Rose Villa was a small cottage with four bedrooms with the rather advanced facility of a bathroom attached to each bedroom. This feature, having a bathroom attached to the bedroom, was a British introduction. Hindu and Parsi homes always had toilets at the rear of the house. Even today, a toilet is referred to as a *pachwara,* back of the house. A veranda encircled the front of the house that overlooked the town. All the doors and windows had minions, an architectural feature considered thrifty and ornamental at the same time. Small pieces of cut glass fitted into these square and triangular patterns and were easy and economical to replace if accidently broken.

Hexagonal tiles covered the floor of Rose Villa, and after the fashion of the time, all the furniture was brought in from Poona and Bombay. Most houses were closed up for the monsoons when schools also sent the children away and most immigrants went back to their hometown and villages to attend to their own small farms. On account of the annual movement between Panchgani and Poona and Bombay, a rather curious system of transportation evolved. While the British travelled by carriageways from the nearest railways station at Meddha or at Poona, the baggage and furniture was loaded on to bullock carts. Carriages made the journey during the day and the bullock carts at night. The bullocks were so used to the long climb up that the cart driver would often go off to sleep and leave it to the animals to make it up by the morning. Milestones on the way marked the distance from the bottom of the Pasarni Ghat (then spelt G-h-a-u-t) and the stones along the edge were cut in such a way that the cartwheels scraped against the cuts. If there was a lull in the scraping sound of the cartwheel against the stone, the driver woke up. There has been no record of any accident ever happening on the bullock cart roads on the Pasarni. The bullocks obviously knew their way.

Life for the British residents travelling in carriages on the ghat was not as easy. The graveyard at St Peter's Church in Panchgani is dotted with graves of both children and adults who died in freak accidents and storms while coming up the Pasarni in the nineteenth century. One such freak accident victim was a British resident who shall forever remain nameless. When you come up the Pasarni, you see a built temple with a little patio on the side. The sign over the doorway of the temple says *Shri Buasaheb Prassana*. The idol is a flat-faced rock painted saffron, the Indian colour for abstinence and other worldliness.

Buasaheb is actually a local corruption of Burra Sahib, an Indian term in British India for white master. Is this the site of an accident in which a British resident had perished? Did his horse slip down the slope from the village of Pasarni while he was out riding? Was he a known figure, a familiar sight on the ghat? Did he lose his way in a storm and his body was never found? Is that why they built a shrine around the site instead of giving him a Christian burial? We have our own way of honouring the dead. The site of the accident was made into a shrine; eyes were painted onto a rock selected to represent him, and he has been given the responsibility of our travels in perpetuity. Just as he was part of the colonising process, we have, by slow process colonised him, our very own British saint.

Panchgani's neighbour, Mahableshwar also has one such saint. A self-appointed caretaker is seen taking care of the statue of Sir Malcolm, the British gentleman who founded Mahableshwar. The bazaar was named Malcolmpeth after him, and his statue is often covered in votive offerings of coconut, flowers, and vermilion. If you ask his devotees who he is and why they are treating him like a Hindu god, they will simply say, 'He takes care of us. We go to him when we have problems.' Mahableshwar's poor have made him their very own collective ancestor. I don't know if there are other such British residents who have been honoured in this manner elsewhere in India. Portuguese India certainly has the most renowned of them all. St Francis Xavier whose mortal remains lie in a silver and glass casket at the Bom Jesus is lovingly called *Goencho Saib* by both Christian and Hindu Goans. They believe that disaster will befall Goa should 'he decide to leave' or his mortal remains moved from the basilica.

We do not know if 'our' Henry Couldrey knew the other British resident, the ghat's Buasaheb. What we do know is that Henry was both cautious and thrifty. He built Rose Villa on a small scale and left the lands as they were found. Leaving Rose Villa on the left, he created a pathway over which he could ride his horses and possibly a carriage up to the loopy land at the end of the plot he had just leased. There, he may have planned to build a bungalow on the same plan as Rose Villa, but unfortunately, he was never able to bring his plans to fruition. Like the system of the time, the bungalow was to be built to the lie of the land. This meant that there were steps that took you to the front of the house that led you to a semi-circular veranda. Once inside the veranda, you entered the formal living room and then the dining room with four bedrooms built around it. By the time you got to the dining area, you realised you were flush against the ground. The back door had no steps at all as the house was built to contour.

A sturdy door opened from the dining room into the pantry where the food from the kitchen was brought in and laid out in chinaware fit for the table. The kitchen was a few metres away from the house across the garden. This kitchen had four rooms set on a high plinth. All the doors opened out towards the house. There were no doors interconnecting the rooms and for a very good reason. A narrow veranda helped movement between rooms and saved men and material in case of a fire. The first room had built-in wood fired stoves, the second had the firewood, the third was for the storage of grain and supplies, and the last one served as a staff room. Stone walls separated one room from the other, also another fire precaution. A covered pathway lined with flat stone tiles enabled staff to carry food platters to the pantry below. The cooked food was laid out on tables in the pantry and then served in the dining room.

Lands in Panchgani were leased in the name of the secretary of state for India 'in Codicil'. Couldrey's plot measured two acres and ten *gunthas*, and Couldrey was charged nine rupees zero paise as annual rent 'at the rate of four rupees per acre'. Lessees were also asked to 'build a substantial bungalow' as a residence on the grounds leased. Lessees were also asked to 'place proper landmarks' marking the boundary of the property and to maintain the same. We do not know why Couldrey never got around to building a larger bungalow. Perhaps he moved back to Bombay or to England much before he had planned to. Even in 1909 when the lease was transferred, Couldrey was not present for the formal signing over of the lease. He was represented by his Attorney John Aikin to whom he had vested all powers.

In 1909, the lease was transferred to a Begum Hurmuttunissa, wife of the Nawab of Wai, Gulam Jilani. The begum purchased the lease about twenty years after Couldrey had acquired it. Just then, India was going through a historic moment. In the year that this lease was transferred from a British resident to an Indian nawab, Mohandas Karamchand Gandhi (not yet referred to as the Mahatma) and his South African companion Hajee Habib had boarded the SS *Kildonan Castle* for Cape Town. Gandhi's eldest son Harilal and several hundred others had already been in South African prisons several times for defying the permit required by all Indians in South Africa. Gopal Krishna Gokhale (and not Gandhi) was the real hero of the *Swaraj* movement, and India was still a long way off from independence. Did Couldrey have a sense of what was brewing under the surface of a smoothly administered British colony? Is that why he chose to sell the lease to an Indian of influence and stature and make his way back home?

One can assume that the nawab's family vacationed in Panchgani, coming up the Pasarni Ghat from the hot rainless plains of Wai. They must have lived in Rose Villa until they decided to build a larger bungalow and decided to get off the main road and move inwards into the land. Much before they built the larger house and before her death, Begum 'Hoormatoonissa' bequeathed the property to Abbasalikahn Mohidin Peerjade, also known as Nawab Abbas Alikhan Goolam Jillani, who began the construction of the main bungalow 'at his own costs and expenses' in or about 1914. The nawab decided to build on the same plan as Rose Villa but to a larger scale. He named the bungalow Abbas Villa, after himself. Despite being owned and constructed by an Indian, the plans and layout of the bungalow and adjacent kitchen and stables are indeed British colonial in design. The nawab's family which comprised his own young family, his brother and his family, and his young sister apparently did not enjoy the new property for more than ten years. The lease changed hands once again in the monsoon of 1924 and came into the hands of a Parsi couple Ardeshir Dossabhoy and his wife Goolbai.

This Parsi couple from Poona (now Pune) and their only daughter Najoo also enjoyed the house as a vacation home. True to style, they kept Rose Villa as it was and added to their acquisition with another bungalow named Rock Side. By now, bungalows in Panchgani were being made all-weather worthy. Instead of closing up houses, residents were enclosing verandas in Panchgani with glass and timber windows and leaving their furniture behind in the hands of caretakers or *malis*. With the coming in of motorcars, horses, and stables were soon replaced by cars, drivers, and garages. It became common practice to turn stables into additional staff quarters. It was also common to keep the caretakers or gardeners and their wives and daughters as staff. Our last caretaker Rajan Jadhav and his family were third-generation employees. Kalu Mali followed by Narayan Jadhav and his wife Abi and later Rajan and his wife Usha had taken care of the property from 1914 to 2004 over three generations.

VIII

Grandmaa . . . Grandma

'Good morning, Pappa. Good morning, Mumma.'

With the caretakers firmly in place, house owners could now leave their furniture and personal belongings in capable hands and leave for the valleys and plains below the ghats. Most residents of Mahableshwar and Panchgani left the hills in the monsoons. For some reason, the Dossabhoys preferred to live in the road fronting Rock Side and rent out both Rose Villa and Abbas Villa. Rose Villa was rented out to a Muslim widow named Marium who lived with her daughter Razia. Abbas Villa was rented by my mother's parents Tehmina and Rustomjee Patell. Tehmina lived in the rented bungalow with a retinue of servants, some local and some that she had herself brought with her from the ancestral home in Siganpore. Petulant and constantly in fear of being at the wrong end of her mother's slippers, Mother spend most of her waking hours with her Sudanese ayah and her Arab cook Yeolett.

It was the year 1928, and Mother was all of six years old. Her stint at the Parsi School had turned out to be a classical boarding school nightmare.

Apparently, it was customary for all the students to line up every morning at breakfast and kiss the principal and his wife and wish them a very good morning by saying, 'Good morning, Pappa. Good morning, Mumma.' An only child, Mother had always had her way. She refused to kiss the couple kicking the old man 'in the wrong place' instead and letting them know that she had her own 'Pappa and Mumma'. She was severely punished for her impunity. She ran away from school in the middle of the night. Yeolett found her asleep under a tree in the morning and refused to allow my grandmother Tehmina to send her to 'such a horrible' school.

She was then placed in the St Joseph's Convent across the road where she was to be groomed into a 'real English lady'. Mother would go to school from the bungalow every morning accompanied by her cook and a rooster and hen pair named Raja and Rani. At school, she learnt to pray to St Anthony, paint on glass, do fretwork with a fret saw, embroider on cushion covers, and make pin cushions out of empty walnut shells. She wore a long dress, bloomers, and a hat on Sundays, played the violin and the mandolin on the front steps, organised fancy dress parties at the house, and when visited by her neighbours, she referred to them as 'Indian'.

Mum is being groomed into a real English lady

By the time Mother was twenty, she had acquired English mannerisms and a Senior Cambridge Certificate with an additional qualification in Domestic Science. Out of the orthodox Zoroastrian atmosphere of the Siganpore house and influenced by the nuns at the St Joseph's Convent, she suddenly discovered religion. While her own mother was attracted to Hindu god men and women, her belief in the miraculous powers of the Christian St Anthony became rock solid. When older, she met with missionaries of a new faith started by the twentieth-century prophet Baha-ullah and began to explore the principles of the Bahai faith. Totally self-taught, she devoured books on religion, philosophy, and English literature.

Something else happened at the house in Panchgani. Ardeshir Dossabhoy, after having acquired three bungalows and over three acres of wooded land, in addition to the large mansion he owned in Poona, realized that he had too much on his plate. Dossabhoy turned the Poona mansion into a dance hall where dance classes were held all day every day of the week. The rents from the two properties in Panchgani were not even enough to pay for repairs to the houses. He began to borrow money. My grandfather Rustomjee was a kind and generous person, but he was also an astute businessman. When Ardeshir asked him for a rather large loan, he asked Ardeshir to mortgage the property. The year was 1942. Ardeshir could not return the loan, and Abbas Villa came to my mother's family.

IX

Grandmother Throws Slippers

'Mui raand,' she screamed, 'Dirty! Dirty! Dirty!'

In another stroke of genius, my grandfather purchased the house in my mother's name instead of keeping it as family property. She was not yet twenty years old and had been described as a student in the sale deed. This act of foresight put my grandmother Tehmina's nose out of joint, and she never forgave her husband. The three of them, mother, father, and only daughter were now living like strangers under one roof. The house gave Mum a voice. It helped her find her feet. Her experiments with the Bahai faith made her into a missionary. She travelled all over southern India with her mentor, living on bread and 'butter balls' as an antidote to hot 'Indian food'. Her father remained mildly amused at this adventure, confident that she would get over it until one day he received an urgent message from the postmaster at the little post office in Panchgani. The postmaster called Rustomjee into his office and showed him the congratulatory telegrams addressed to his daughter. Mother had adopted the Bahai faith. Manijeh

Rustomjee Patell had become a Bahai. This shattered my grandfather. He was heartbroken. I personally think he would have forgiven her if she had told him herself. But to hear the news from the postmaster of the town post office was more than he could take.

Grandmother had always been a jealous mother, always competing with her daughter for her husband's attentions. She had always wanted a son and had wept when several of her male children had died at birth. I don't suppose anyone had heard of the G6PD gene or the Rh+ blood group and its associated health risks back then. She resented Mother simply because she, a girl, had survived, while her 'beautiful boys' had perished. Perhaps to compensate for this hatred, Grandfather had been a doting father. He had done everything that normally a mother would do.

He had encouraged her to read when he himself had never had had a chance to study and could read and write only in Gujarati and study music. He would bring back samples of nail varnish from the store in Aden and help Mother colour her nails as they giggled and laughed in the Panchgani afternoons. When she first got her period, Grandmother took the flat leather *sapat* off her foot and threw it at her daughter. '*Mui raand*,' she screamed, 'Dirty! Dirty! Dirty!' It was Grandfather who taught her how to make a sanitary pad from clean rags, laughing all the while and putting the terrified girl at ease. '*Mui raand*' in Parsi Gujarati simply means cursed whore.

Grandfather did not take the news of the conversion well. Rustomjee left for Aden in a huff, and Grandmother Tehmina left for her other home in Bandra, Bombay. Mother had obviously made it known that she did not need to be supervised by her parents anymore. An only child, the house in Panchgani became her best friend and surrogate sibling. She put Abbas Villa to work. Along with eight other Bahai friends, she started the New Era School in Panchgani in a small house on the lower slopes of the town. As a schoolgirl, she had saved her weekly pocket money of Rs 5 and had bought a small house in Dhobi Gully for what was then a handsome sum of Rs 5,000. The rent from that house was her only source of income then.

Her parents had left her to fend for herself as a direct reprimand for her conversion. The school did not have any money to pay its teachers a salary.

Undaunted by her new state of penury and with new students who could not afford school fees, the front garden of her home became a farm. They were soon growing greens for the table. The house also became a home for the teachers who came from outside Panchgani. Together, they planted cabbages and broad beans and rejoiced when the three jackfruit trees bore fruit. Kalu Mali kept buffaloes, and they were never short of milk. Wild raspberries and mulberries were saved as special treats. Life was not without its dramatic moments. When they saw a snake in the house, they would call their neighbour Kishan Jankar who had a gun license. With Kishan's unique manner of handling the reptiles, it's a small wonder that anyone even lived to tell the tale.

The house becomes Mum's best friend

The number of students soon went up, and some paying students joined the school, and it grew to a full-fledged residential establishment of a very high educational standard. Mother and her fellow teachers caught up with their embroidery, crotchet, and painting on holidays. After her complete transformation from a barefoot village school girl at the Siganpore Gujarati School to a white stocking teacher's pet of Sister Mary Alban at the St. Joseph's Convent in Panchgani, Mother went in the 'wrong direction' once again. She began to take an interest in Indian philosophy, Sufism, and Hindustani Classical music. She began to compose and sing Sufi *qawalis*. Having no one else in Panchgani who she could sing with, she began to sing with the locals. The large ballroom at Abbas Villa soon became the stage for their *mehfils*. Mother was so involved in the music that she ignored the social system of the time and saw nothing wrong in befriending the town's *dhobis*, butchers, and mechanics some of who were Muslims. She grew her hair long, took to wearing cotton saris and sturdy leather *chappals* made in Kolhapur. Her parents maintained a stony silence right through this period of defiance.

Another great change was to take place. As soon as my parents got married, the *qawalis* gave way to ballroom dancing. Social life at the house was abuzz with wine, lavish dinners, and Western Classical music. In a typical Victorian hangover, we children were allowed to stay up for the parties until it was our 'bedtime at 8'. For the *qawali* nights, however, the Indian system of allowing children to stay up until the last guest had left or until they dropped dead from exhaustion prevailed. For both events, however, the rule was that children 'should be seen, not heard'.

Abbas Villa had stood by Mother while she struggled in Panchgani. The house had helped her stand alone, defiant and engaged in what was then considered the most 'noble' of professions, teaching. It had provided food and given her and her friends safety, shelter, and dignity. Grandmother was an acclaimed narcissist. For her, everything was always either about self-preservation or about Zoroastrian piety. Mother, on the other hand, lived for the community and for a new world religion. Grandmother had once refused to help a man lying injured on the Pasarni Ghat. '*Gaadi kharab thai jasey*' (The car will get ruined), she had said. Mother had opened her home and her heart in a completely unprecedented show of faith in humanity. She had loved the house since her school days and the house loved her back, becoming her safety net, her comfort, and her soulmate.

X

Working with Dr Jane Goodall

'It must be like a wedding.'

I went to Tanzania under rather strange circumstances. The story begins in Vadodara, then Baroda, and growing up in Number 14, Officers Colony. I was sixteen and in love with 'the boy next door'. The boy, Prashant Pandit, an engineering student, happened to come from a Gujarati Brahmin family. My parents, themselves a mixed couple, vehemently objected to my 'going steady' with a Gujarati, a 'non-Parsi', and did their best to dissuade me from harbouring any thoughts of marrying him.

The colony we lived in was made up of Gujarati families. How did they expect this not to have happened? The Parsis in Baroda shunned us because Dad was a 'non'. The children in the colony and at school were our only friends. At sixteen, when I got the attention every teenager seeks from her neighbour's son, I was flattered. In my short dresses, hipster skirts, and halter necklines, it was I who looked exotic to the tradition-bound Gujarati boys in the neighbourhood. Prashant and I fell in love.

Prashant was the youngest of four siblings, all of who wanted to leave the small provincial town and 'go abroad'. Prashant's sisters married and left (one for Kenya and the other for Tanzania), and Prashant, westernised by the standard of the day, was simply waiting his turn. When my mother and father saw that there was little they could do to break my friendship with the family, they schemed. They encouraged me to apply for a post graduate degree in the United Kingdom. That, they thought, would end the friendship. Who knew what would happen when I went abroad? I might even meet someone interesting (perhaps white) and forget about the Gujarati boy next door.

It was the decade of India's notorious brain drain. All my school friends had either found husbands in America or admissions in colleges in the United Kingdom. I chose to apply to the University of Birmingham. Unknown to my parents, Prashant's sister Lena had escaped from an oppressive marriage in Kenya and had come to Birmingham with her young son Neil. I would go to Birmingham, I thought, close to people who would one day be my family.

Very soon, we were all playing a game that would change our lives forever. Prashant insisted that we get officially engaged before I leave. He also said that he would 'allow' me to leave only on the condition that I would make arrangements for him to follow. I agreed to both conditions, thinking that perhaps this was the only way to escape from a landscape of reality to a land of dreams. I took Mother on a drive in our aquamarine Ambassador and stopped the car in a wooded area in which I knew we would both be comfortable for the 'talk'. I proposed that Prashant and I get engaged in a public reception. 'It must be like a wedding.' Reluctantly, my mother agreed as long as it was an engagement and not a wedding. There was nothing legal or sacrosanct about an engagement after all.

I lasted at the Birmingham University dormitory for exactly three days. Lena came to see me, but I had no idea of how seriously involved I was with her brother. Never having lived on my own and never having had to fend for myself, I went through the humiliating experience of begging my dorm mates for food over the weekend because the banks were closed. I simply did not know how to cope. I called my brother's friend Chandu Shah in London. Chandu and his wife Bharati asked me to come and stay with them in West Harrow if I 'did not like it there'. I packed my bag, my first experience with a luggage novelty – moulded bag with two castors, and left without letting anyone know either at the university office or the dorm. I had not yet paid my school fees, and if there were any dues at the dorm, I still owe them the money.

My tuition fees stayed parked in the bank, and I began to do odd jobs in London to pay Chandu and Bharati for the small box room that they had given me to stay. I worked in canteens and cafes so that there were always scones, sandwiches, and muffins that I could bring home for tea. Over weekends, Chandu and I would go visit Indian friends and do odd jobs for them. I learnt how to paper walls, lay carpets, and polish banisters there. Nothing gave us more pleasure than working on houses. Prashant would make expensive calls from India, and I still remember the shrill ringing that would echo through Chandu's three-bedroom 'semi-detached' with the snow lining the windows and the season's first daffodils, flawlessly perfect, nodding in the fresh breezes of a new spring. There were no mobiles those days, and everyone in the house heard every word of your conversation. Prashant had finished his post-graduation in Structural Engineering, and he was now ready for England.

Still in our teens, underexposed to the ways of the world and immigration laws, we made plans for Prashant to fly to England on a tourist visa. He was firm in the belief that since we were part of the Commonwealth, we were 'almost British'. I sent him a ticket, bought with the money my parents had given me for my tuition fees, and Prashant set his sights on his trip. Naturally, he was stopped at immigration and not allowed into the country. I visited him in detention every single day, teary-eyed and clueless. Since he had flown Alitalia, he was given two choices: he could either fly to Rome or go back to India. We chose Rome. It was the summer of 1978. Rome and the Vatican became our home for two weeks. It was our very own Roman holiday. We spent all our money on pizzas and giant carafes of cheap red wine, leaving us with just enough to fly back to Bombay.

'I can't bear to go back to India,' Prashant said. We began to think about what else we could do. The man we used to buy pizzas from spoke no English, and we knew no Italian. To this day, I do not know how we managed to communicate with him, but he gave us a flier with an address on it. Someone was looking for people to house-sit their cat. We used the doorbell, buzzer and sign language, and managed to get a large room with lots of character (read clutter) in the heart of the city. Poochi would visit once a day for his food, and we learnt how to say, 'Poochi! *Avanti!*' We took photos, and we talked about the future. I suddenly thought of Pushpa. She had been the other guest at Chandu's place. Pushpa was from Tanzania and had talked a lot about her homeland. Prashant had heard a lot about Tanzania from his sister Nina and her husband Hemant Kumar. One of our friends from Baroda had also gone there recently to help an uncle run his hardware store. Nainesh would be there. Everyone we knew had had a wonderful stay there. At the count of three, we took an Alitalia flight to Dar es Salaam.

There was a light drizzle when we landed at the airport. I can still see the huge mango trees stirring in the African breeze. There were no friendly posters at the airport. There were no signs saying, 'WELCOME TO TANZANIA', the land of your dreams. I had spent a year in England, pretending to my parents and myself that I had gone there to study advertising. All I was learning there was how not to go back. And that is how we had landed in this East African country. Immigration would not clear us because we had 'no purpose' for our visit. We were to be put on the next flight back to Bombay. All the other Indian passengers had left for their homes. We looked different. Africa! All I will ever see of this continent will be a steel bench, peeling paint on the walls, and my own luggage strewn on the floor, I thought. I had to do something.

We were waiting on the stainless steel bench, despondent. I suppose we were waiting for an angel, a miracle, anything. It came in the shape and uniform of an Alitalia ground manager, portly and pink, at the airport. He walked up to us and asked us a few questions. Had we come on a visit?

Did we have a tourist visa? Was there anyone in Tanzania that we knew socially? Did we have an address? Where were we planning to stay? Were we planning to stay on? Did we have any money to spend here? He spoke to immigration in the local Swahili, and soon we were in an Alitalia official car on our way into Dar es Salaam in the rain, chatting all the way with our Alitalia benefactor. Had I seen an African lion? he had asked. Had I seen a giraffe or wildebeest? Had I ever been out on the Serengeti Plains?

He soon realized that we were not exactly luxury hotel material and dropped us off at a cheap hotel in the city. Our room was full of cockroaches. And Dar es Salaam was not as small a town as we thought it would be. We did not know where Nainesh lived or worked and had no address for him. 'He's got to be there somewhere.' I took a shower as quickly as the bathroom cockroaches would allow and walked towards a compound wall where I saw some boys shooting the breeze just like they did in Baroda and most other Gujarat towns. They were absolutely shocked to see an Indian woman in a dress, walking towards them and addressing them directly. 'No, we do not know a Nainesh Patel. No, we have not heard of anyone who had come to Tanzania from Baroda recently.' One of the boys must have seen the crestfallen expression on my face and suggested that I go to the Patel Club to look for our friend. 'Every community here has its own club,' he suggested. 'All the Patels meet at the Patel Club every evening.'

Prashant had lost all hope by then and began to look at his engineering degree. We walked to the Patel Club and asked for Nainesh. No one had heard of him. They asked us if we knew the uncle's name and then began to wonder where we really had come from. I began to describe Nainesh to them, and someone said, 'Oh, they are looking for the *bhania*, the Nephew!' Nainesh had come to work with his uncle and it was natural therefore to address him as 'Nephew'. No one had bothered to ask the nephew what his real name was. Neither Uncle nor Nephew was there at the Club that evening but the others offered to let Nainesh know that we were looking for them. Nainesh was completely surprised to see us and quickly rescued us from the hotel and took us to see his uncle, cousins, more uncles, and aunts, all of who made us feel more than welcome in the land of their adoption.

Not once did anyone ask how we got to Tanzania, where we were from, or what religion we followed. In fact, they did not even ask if we were married to each other. Just the fact that Nainesh or 'Nephew' had known us from India was enough to get us into homes, on dinner tables, and job interviews. In those days, people in Dar es Salaam travelled a lot. Someone or the other was always on their way to England or India. Safety from burglaries and break-ins was a constant concern when you were away. A system of house-sitting had evolved over the years that they called 'house-warming'. Never a stickler for the English Grammar, we offered to house-sit for anyone who had to leave town. We soon became Dar's most popular 'house warmers'.

Prashant and I become Dar's most popular house warmers

The Indians in East Africa had come there to build the railways 150 years ago. As they settled into remote pockets of the country, they began to do what they did best. They opened small *dukas* or shops and supplied stores to Indian, African, and British households. If there was one word that described how *muhindi* or Indian bosses treated black African workers, it was 'cruelly'. Some *banianis* paid their black African workers in sacks of rice and salt or bolts of fabric. An African servant was expected to stand all day in the store, cook and clean for his employer, and sleep on the floor of the store doubling up as security guard for the night. If he received one decent meal at the end of the day, he considered himself lucky.

To the Asian in the 1960s in Tanzania, the black African was the face that stopped you at the airport, the hand that checked the numbers on the engine of your car and asked you if the car was stolen, and the eyes that peered at papers held upside down. In the early 1970s, however, the African Tanzanians got a chance to see a different Indian. Educated Asian doctors, nurses, teachers, and computer programmers from India and Pakistan were working in Tanzanian hospitals, offices, banks, and post offices. Then there were the Asian engineers who built the bridges, roads, and office high rises, the new, modern Tanzania. This was an Asian quite different from the sacks of salt and bolts of cloth Asian *bania*. This new Asian kept to himself after office hours and treated the African with respect due to a colleague at work. This Asian was less equal than the equals; he was not rich. There was an element of surprise when this Asian opened his mouth to speak English at work and even more surprise when he actually put in an honest day's work at the construction site.

The informal segregation in Tanzania was Africa's best kept secret. Asian, European, and African lived in their own segregated 'quarters' reminiscent of Black Town, White Town, Native Town, and so on as in British Bombay. The Asian quarter in Dar es Salaam was called Upanga. It was in the heart of the city, where chubby Asian schoolboys cut across lines to watch parades at the Upanga Police Station parade grounds. The expats, Indian, Pakistani, and European, all lived along the waterfront, far from the central business district in well-appointed bungalows with imposing front gates, black African security guards, and dogs. Most dogs were chained or caged during the day, given raw meat, and then let free at night. Only the most desperate would dare invade.

Most Indians in East Africa had come from Gujarat. The dhows they were crammed in took over three months to make the journey. A hole at the end of the stern served as open toilet. Meals on board were coarse rice and *dhal*. Travel speed depended on the wind and sometimes dhows would have to wait for days under a baking hot sky for the wind to turn. There was no cover. With their bodies covered in lice and their hearts swelling with hope and anticipation, they often ended up working for relatives who had settled in a little earlier. In financial debts before they had set sail, they would try and pay back with what little they earned. Curiously, once their own positions were secure, they themselves became the exploiters and oppressors of the new migrants that came.

The Gujaratis in Tanzania were an integral part of the Indian Diaspora in East Africa. Everyone you met invariably said, 'We're not planning to live here. We'll just make a little bit and then leave for . . .' the unsaid blank for you to fill in with the country of your choice. A lot of them were sending money home to India to build houses, finance shops, or set up small businesses. Some were sending money to England where they had relatives who would manage their investments. The funny thing was that this feeling of temporariness, of 'not belonging here', was handed down from generation to generation, over close to a hundred and fifty years. They all lived like they would in their hometowns and villages, ate, dressed, and celebrated their weddings just like they would do back home, had Tanzanian or British passports, and yet never once did we hear anyone speak of Tanzania affectionately.

No Indian in Tanzania ever called the country home. Most held dual passports, most had one foot either in India or in the UK. Every Indian expected to be expelled at a moment's notice and hence, figuratively speaking, ran on gilded shoes. They lived in cramped three storied buildings, families bunching together and hanging on to one common refrain: why build better homes here? '*Amarey kya ahin rehvanoo chey*', we're not planning to live here forever. How could you think of yourself a stranger when you had spent over 150 years in a country? When you had raised sons and married off daughters and set up businesses so successful that you could stash away funds in the Bank of England overseas?

Prashant soon found a job with a Gujarati stone quarry owner, and I began working in the same office looking after the accounts. When we both found jobs in Dar es Salaam, we applied for the right kind of visas that allowed us to work. The company had given us a small house to live in and an old Fiat to run around town. There was still something missing, though, to make us feel that we belonged. We were not part of a club. There was the Patel Club, the Luana Club, and the Vania Club, but none of these were open to our combination of Brahmin boy and half-Parsi girl. The Parsis in Dar were too few in number to have a club of their own. I think they were all of twenty-three in number, including the ones who lived in Zanzibar.

In the community of Gujaratis in Tanzania, I did not belong. Prashant did not want to belong. Sensing our awkwardness in the community of Patels, Nainesh introduced us to the Parsis in Tanzania. Most Parsis here, he said, drank alcohol and told funny stories. I would fit in perfectly. As if on cue, the Parsis in Tanzania decided to adopt us immediately. The fact that my parents had opposed our match and had sent me off to England to precipitate a break up with Prashant added to the sympathy factor. Miles away from home, rejected as a couple by parents and siblings, and never having been made to feel a part of the Parsi community in Baroda, we now had several sets of Parsi foster parents, patrons, well-wishers, and benefactors in faraway Africa.

Our circle of new friends grew. We were in a whirlwind of parties, dinners, and lunches in Parsi homes. And then, we met Tim David. Novices at everything, especially handling a car without parental supervision, we were out on a Sunday drive when the little engine of our company Fiat seized. Those were the days when you checked the levels of the engine oil, brake oil, and gear oil. We only knew how to turn a key and drive. There was not a drop of oil in the engine, and thick black smoke was spewing out of the front of the car. Typically, we left the car where it was and were wondering what to do when we saw a tall fair-skinned man walking his dog. 'Hello,' he said, 'what seems to be the problem?' We explained what had happened, and he quietly suggested we park the little Fiat in his compound for the night. The three of us pushed the car with his little dachshund Pip yapping away at the tyres. It was the start of a lifelong friendship.

Prashant went to collect the car the following day; Tim invited him in for a cup of tea and then began to tell him about his work at the office of the British High Commission. One thing led to another and soon Tim David, first officer at the British High Commission was a regular visitor at our company house, enjoying the Indian food at our modest table and the company of our Parsi friends in Tanzania. There was no official segregation in East Africa, and people could mix socially. Tanzania, when it was Tanganyika and Zanzibar, had been a British Protectorate. Although the twenty-three members of the Parsi community in Dar es Salaam had taken us under their wing and made us part of their lives, we were acutely aware that we had a past. We had come to Tanzania by default. We had dreams of living in England amongst the daffodils of our school poems and the 'hills and dales' of our literature lessons. When Tim befriended us, it was as if we had come close to literature.

Tim was a bachelor then (Rosie and the two children were to come in the future), and we often helped him out with his parties. Wives of 'embassy husbands' worked in the embassies and consulates in those days. Even if they carried little black boxes of confidential papers from one floor to another while their husbands held meetings with Tanzanian and Ghanaian businessmen, it was an embassy job. In the evenings, everyone without exception, even those wives who had never had any experience with servants, complained about the 'native servants'. The newer the wife was to the system, the longer the complaint. The Tanzanian heard all this with characteristic stoic. They got their own kicks by giving their mistresses colourful nicknames.

Dr Jane Goodall, for example, became Mama Mkubwa or the great and wonderful lady. I was Mama Mdogo or the little lady. My friend Sherna was named Mama Sigara because she smoked and Toni Breschia, who carried his short and stocky frame in and out of the ships that operated on the lake, became Bwana Toni Mfupi or the short master Toni. A Hindu guest would often be referred to as the Mama Baniani and her husband Bwana Mkubwa. Bania would strictly apply to the caste of traders and merchants, but here the Tanzanian knew no different. To him, every Indian was a keeper of shops.

The Tanzanian was a tough worker. Tough, that is, until he fainted at the sight of blood. Big built gardeners would hack away at woody or thorny bushes in the hot Equatorial sun, but one single pin prick could bring them down to their knees. 'Do you know why I drink so much?' asked a well-known Tanzanian surgeon once. 'Because I can't stand the sight of blood.' His Indian obstetrician counterpart once confessed that at the government hospital where he worked, there was no relief for the Indian doctors. When it came to the first few babies, he said, he could follow all the text book procedures. As the night advanced and he had done more than ten deliveries and there was no help from his African colleagues, he would just stand and watch and let Mother Nature do her best. The poor screaming mother-to-be could be in a corn field under the stars for all anyone cared.

Even after they arrived, Tanzanian babies hardly seemed to be any trouble at all. They were delivered, nursed, and then left with aging grandparents in the village. This left the parents to live and work in the cities. Like chimp families, a Tanzanian family was mother and babies. And a Tanzanian mother came bearing the scent of beer, *ugali*, and beans, the staple for most East Africans. *Ugali* is a stiff porridge made with corn meal with stewed kidney beans and the occasional sliver of meat. For the babies, it was *ugali* softened to make an easy-to-digest feed. If you, an outsider, chose to eat *ugali* or did your hair up in braids or spoke to a non-African in Swahili, you became an instant social outcast. People would have found one more reason to exclude you and treat you as a 'non'.

Unlike in neighbouring South Africa, here, in Tanzania, there was no 'official racism' or any hint of apartheid. President Julius Nyerere had a careful mix of cosmopolitan members in his own Cabinet. It was almost as if Mwalimu's Cabinet was on show for the world to see how multiracial and broadminded Tanzania was. In fact, people congregated within their religious or racial communities exclusively, and social interaction between communities was restricted to the work place. I still cannot remember how we met up with people from various parts of the world. Perhaps it was Tim who introduced us to the other 'expats' in Tanzania. It might have also been some of our Parsi friends who had actually come to work in Tanzania from England or Pakistan and had come with no racist baggage. Prashant's work brought him into contact with other engineers from all over the world. We were in and out of one another's homes.

Some homes had funny stories coming out of their brick walls. This Nigerian friend of ours from Lagos kept two homes. One was a grand house when he entertained friends officially with his 'official wife' as hostess. The other was a small cottage where friends like us would drop in unannounced to catch up with him and his Tanzanian girlfriend. Needless to say, he also kept two cars. When he went out with his Nigerian wife, he took the silver Mercedes, and when he went out with his Tanzanian girlfriend, he took the Mini. A big car could attract attention.

There was a similar story in the home of a Tanzanian minister. He had a house with a grand staircase in the centre. The staircase divided his two houses, one to the left and the other to the right. 'Welcome! Welcome!' the Cabinet Minister would say. 'Would you like to meet my cows?' He would then point you in the direction of his wives' houses in turns, referring to them as cows all the while praising their 'productivity'. By this time we would be laughing so much we never found out how many children he had. Quite honestly, I doubt if even he knew how many children there were in the house or even how many of those children were his own.

Our Nigerian friend's Tanzanian girlfriend would sometimes walk in with as many as seven children of various colour combinations, shapes, and sizes. When asked what their names were she would say, 'Oh, that's coffee, that is chocolate, that is coffee with cream, that is coffee with too much cream . . .' and so on. None of the children resembled our Nigerian friend, and when they needed to spend some quiet time together, she would take all her children and leave them with 'one of my mothers in the village'. It is only in Africa that you can accomplish such a biological feat. You could have more than one mother because all your father's wives and mistresses are 'mothers'. Most 'mothers' got along with one another, and the best part was that any 'mother' could be asked to fill in as grandmother.

Prashant and I got married because we had to. Prashant's employers, good old-fashioned Gujaratis, would not give us the company house to live in if we were not 'officially married'. One morning, I took a bus in my checked shirt and beige skirt and got off at the marriage registrar's office. Prashant came in the company car straight from work. Two of our friends, Homi and Harish, signed as witnesses, and we were married. We giggled through the entire procedure.

Social life for us was interesting and rich, but we were not enjoying our work. Tim warned us, in proper English fashion, against having all our eggs in one basket. We were both working for the same company, our house was given to us by our Indian employer, and so was the car. Tim gave us the courage give up our jobs, house, and car. He asked us to house-sit for him while he was away on holiday. Although he had security guards and cooks and a maid who could take care of things while he was in the UK, I think he felt more comfortable that way. Besides, it also gave us the opportunity to look at job options.

Tim was convinced that his house staff was spying on him. He did not think there was anything extraordinary about it, and I took it all with a pinch of salt. Then something happened. We had moved into his house with every stitch we owned which was not much considering the circumstances. I did have a few dollars in cash and a few hundred English pounds that I had managed to save from my leanings in England. I had them in a combination safe in the cupboard in the guest room. They had been sealed in an envelope. One morning when I went to the safe and took the envelope out, the seal was intact but the money was gone. In its place was a wad of white paper, the kind they used as stationery in the British

Consulate. When Tim came back and I told him what had happened, he seemed sad but not surprised.

I became Tim David's official host at the consulate bungalow. I learnt how to do things his way, ordering Philadelphia cream cheese and caviar from England in the diplomatic pouch and handing tubes of English cheddar to his English friends who were 'simply starving' for bread and cheese. Marooned in prawn-and-peaches country, we all craved the food we were born in. It was amongst these English 'expats' that I met Rosie Frith. Rosie was working for Dr Jane Goodall at a chimpanzee research station at a wildlife reserve called Gombe along Lake Tanganyika. She was Jane's field and research assistant and went with Jane to the research station every fortnight. When she was not at the station, she spent her time with her English boyfriend in Dar es Salaam.

One afternoon, I walked in to see Rosie in tears with Tim handing her a generous supply of face tissues. 'My boyfriend is leaving for Reed, and Jane won't let me leave unless I find a replacement.' Tim and I looked at each other. Where was the problem? I had a degree in Statistics from the MS University of Baroda, and Rosie took me to see Jane. My first meeting with Jane was like that of two friends who had not seen each other for a long time. There was some awkwardness on my part and a little deliberately kept distance on hers. Rosie must have said her prayers that day, and I got the job.

She followed her boyfriend to England, and Prashant and I moved into Jane's beach house originally meant for Dr Derek Bryceson's mother, Jane's mother-in-law, who unfortunately never lived to see it. Derek was a close friend of President Mwalimu and the only 'white' member of Mwalimu's Cabinet. At high tide, the sea washed our front lawn. Fish vendors came to our French windows facing the ocean with fresh catches of lobsters that were still alive. Monitor lizards as big as the sofas played tag in our living room. We shared a compound wall with the president of the country.

Friends amongst the Asian community were thrilled. They couldn't believe our luck. The Gujarati set wondered what I was supposed to be doing in a park filled with 'monkeys' surrounded by *karias,* blacks. A family

I had met and stayed with wondered if I would be safe in the forest with only 'blacks' for company.

It was my first trip out into the unknown. Jane and I were to fly to Kigoma, and from there we were to take a boat to our camp on the edge of the second largest freshwater lake in the world. I was looking forward to seeing the chimpanzees. My Gujarati friends were so anxious that they made me promise that we would stay the night in Kigoma with some friends who had been running the local store there for decades. Jane was bemused by the whole Indian drama unfolding before her. She had come to Gombe as a young girl with her mother and Dr Leakey at first and then later as an independent researcher herself. She had camped in the Gombe forests under the stars. She had followed chimps up and down the thickly forested hill slopes all by herself, had baked bread in makeshift ovens dug out of ground dirt, and had bathed in the lake under the watchful eye of spitting cobras and water snakes. 'No one has ever worried about me,' she joked.

We spent a comfortable night at the Gujarati household. Before we went to bed, we were told not to stir out of the room once the dogs were let out of their cages. Vegetarian themselves, this family had their five German shepherds fed on raw meat and kept them locked up all day only to be let out at night. Kigoma, like the rest of Tanzania, had a high crime rate. It was a curious situation where even the owners of the house could not trust their own dogs. Guard dogs were known to tear owners to pieces if they ventured out of their rooms at night. Jane and I left for Gombe the following morning in a commercial motor boat where half the population was wearing real fur coats. The scenery we whizzed past was spell-binding. Jane and I smiled at everything and everyone we saw.

Lake Tanganyika washes the borders of Tanzania and Zaire (former Belgian Congo), and as we jostled shoulders with our fellow Zairian passengers, Jane cheerfully filled me in with stories of how four American students from Stanford University had been kidnapped by Zaire rebels a few years ago. The American students had been treated well and spoke highly of their abductors when they were finally set free. She reassured me that there was no need to be afraid. *Of course*, I said to myself, *who would pay ransom for an unknown Indian?* I fortunately lived in an era where everyone from America was rich and anyone from India was poor. 'However, as a precaution,' Jane said, 'we'll just sleep in our clothes.' I readily agreed. After all, who wanted to get kidnapped in their pyjamas?

I saw my first pair of Pallas's fishing eagles by the lake as we sailed past. When we landed, I saw my first spitting cobra, my first twig snake, and my first pair of leopards. In the absence of Internet or mobile phones, I had come to the field without having done any background research. Jane took me to the forest 'feeding station' straightaway. Great big bunches of bananas, in various shades of green and yellow, had been placed in a concrete bunker with small windows from where the chimps could pick their share. Jane and I were to sit behind the trees and pretend to be invisible. With clipboard and pen in hand, we were to record our observations of wild chimpanzee behaviour 'every minute on the minute'. As the groups or individual chimps left, we were to pick our 'target' chimp and follow him/her or them and record their social behaviour on our printed sheets.

Jane walked with me on my first day. We were soon face to face with a group of chimp mothers and children. I instinctively turned my back to what looked to me like an alpha female. She brushed past me with a grunt. Jane smiled. My training as Dr Jane Goodall Bryceson's field and research assistant had begun. As we walked that morning up and down the forested hill slopes, Jane showed me how to avoid the deep ravines and crevices. 'One of my research assistants went through a crevice here, and her body was never found.' She also told me to avoid following the males and let the Tanzanian field assistants do that instead. 'Their range is wider and can extend to over twenty-five kilometres in a day. They also go up the steeper slopes. And they're much faster than the females.' I should keep to following females with their babies. 'They move at a slower pace and also stop to eat quite often.'

Jane was in the middle of telling me how female chimps will sometimes pick a 'tool', a long blade of grass, to use later as a fishing rod and fish for termites at a termite mound. Chimp females often travelled with other mothers and children and sometimes with their own grown daughters. Here I was in familiar territory. In India, your mother's sisters or *maasis* often took over from your mother in caregiving. It was the same with the chimpanzees. That they used tools to fish for termites was fascinating to watch, but what was more interesting was the fact that they actually collected the tools and walked a considerable distance to the termite mound. Chimpanzees could actually plan a fishing trip.

Chimps pick their tools much before the fishing trip

The other thing that fascinated me on my first trip to Gombe was the way the chimps could hide themselves up in a tree. They generally made grunting sounds and communicated with one another almost all the time, but when they did not want *you* to know they were there, they were as quiet as any chimpanzee could be. You could walk past a whole family of chimps feeding on ripe palm nuts up in a palm tree and not know it. They normally allowed the nuts to fall to the ground when they were eating, but when they saw you from a distance, they actually quietly tucked the nuts into the crown of the tree. That way falling nuts would not give the game away.

You could walk past a family of chimps and not know it

Jane talked all the way as we went along, and just when I thought she had warned me about every single danger ('Twig snakes look like twigs but they are fatal so be careful when you crawl under the bushes') at day or night ('Leopards hunt the baboons at dusk. Make sure you don't get in the way') I heard a growl, and someone really large thumped me on my back. Jane laughed out loud as I went to the bottom of the slope with my head in my hands. 'Never make eye contact with a male. Never forget that you are female. They take it as a challenge.' I had met my first male chauvinist.

Comfort came in the form of two ripe bananas and a boiled egg for lunch. We began to walk again following a new set of target chimpanzees. Some of the chimps are really funny with their bananas. They come to the feeding station, gingerly pick a few, and then tuck them in between their feet. They peel one and eat the fruit, then scrape the inside of the banana peel, and then eat the rest of the peel. Why eat the fruit in three stages when you can do it in one? They were also very funny when it rained. They would sometimes fashion a neat little umbrella with a large palm frond or leaf. They would hold the 'umbrella' over their heads. When it rained harder and the little umbrella became useless, they would simply throw it on the ground and give up, getting soaked to the skin.

At the end of our day, we showered in the lake with fish nibbling at our feet. 'Don't move if you see a water snake. They are deadly poisonous.' We got dressed in our jungle green shirt and trousers. 'We're better off sleeping in our clothes. Can you hear the engine of the motor boat passing by? We heard the same kind of rattling and throbbing when the kidnappers came.' Lake Tanganyika was so expansive, it was like bathing in the ocean. There was our shingle beach where our camp stood and then there was nothing but clear water on all sides. Our camp was a concrete block with three large rooms and chicken mesh for windows. The papers we were working on, the data sheets that were filled in by our eleven Swahili field assistants, and a few books lay scattered in the first room where we sat on old sofas with some of the stuffing missing. The other two rooms had the beds. Our toilet, a dug out latrine with a 'western-style' commode perched on the top, was outside our camp house.

We waited for the last boat to go past with its cargo of fur-clad passengers. We jumped into the lake for our showers, using no soap for fear of polluting the water. Our clothes, left on the shingle beach to dry off, had to be guarded against curious baboons on their way into the forest for the night. Once we had dried off and were in our green fatigues, dressed for the following day, we were ready for dinner. Jane brought out a tin of baked beans and some potatoes. We made a stove with some flat stones and a wire mesh that served as burner. Like the chimps, we too had collected a few sticks for a cooking fire on our way back from 'work'. Jane showed me how to use the small twigs as tinder and how to manage the fire under the cooking pots. The potatoes we baked directly in the embers, the saucepan with the beans over the mesh. For dessert, we fried a few bananas in bright red palm oil in a frypan and then drizzled them with some sugar to caramelise them evenly. It was a meal you could never forget.

I make a meal at Gombe

There was no electricity at Gombe so we had to finish our washing up and clearing up, our showers, and our laundry, our last trip to the toilet before it got dark. Once in bed with our fatigues on, we listened to the lapping of the waves on the beach and passing motor boats until we fell asleep. Following chimpanzees from seven in the morning to seven at night, taking a banana break for lunch, and coming back to cook our meagre meal over a wood-fired wire mesh stove soon became routine. On account of the history of the kidnapping of the American students, Mwalimu had made it a rule that no researcher would be allowed to stay in national parks and sanctuaries for more than fifteen days at a stretch. So we were to spend fifteen days at Gombe and the other two weeks back in Dar es Salaam. It was a good arrangement except that leaving parcels of food in the freezer at the beach house for Prashant put a toll on our already stormy relationship.

Working with Jane Goodall, living in a beach house in such close proximity to both Mwalimu and Derek, a member of Mwalimu's Cabinet, gave both Prashant and me a lot of social leverage. On Sundays, our social set would come over for a pot luck party, and we often went on runs on the beach or rides in someone's dune buggy. Prashant and I began to grow apart as I began to prefer the company of animals to that of humans. 'So? Has a male chimpanzee made a pass at you yet?' In Tanzania, you can divorce your wife for two reasons: one, if she cannot cook and the other, if she is no good in bed. Prashant chose the first option.

When I left Tanzania in July 1981, I left with the memory of crabs on the beach, crowned cranes on the sands, fishing boats with their lights on to attract the catch, and the dramatic beauty of a thunderstorm on the sea. Most of the Africa I had seen was flat. There were the mountains in the north of course, Mt Meru and the southern flank of Mt Kilimanjaro. The vast plains of the Serengeti from where thousands of animals migrated had been cut up into two countries; Kenya and Tanzania shared a border but no social relations.

When my friend Sherna Wadia 'Mama Sigara' visited my mother in Bandra and gave her an update on the trouble that Prashant and I were having in Tanzania, she decided to take a flight to Africa and help patch things up. When she gave up on the mediation, we decided to go on an African safari before flying back to Bombay. And although Kenya and Tanzania shared a border but no border relations, they still had the same mountain and the same safari traditions. Every room in the safari lodge, for example, had a copy of the Holy Bible on the bedside table. Every room had a huge picture window from where you could see gazelles, marabou storks at the lodge garbage dumps, and elephants on the slopes.

Red sunlight bathed the red plains of the Serengeti as two young elephants sparred in mock combat. The sides of the craters had huge gashes where the elephants had mined the hillside for rock salt. No two zebras looked alike. While the Europeans and Indians said the zebra stripes were black on white, the African insisted they were white on black. Light grey clouds parted in places and gave way to a grey whiteness. It was rather like an artist pausing over a piece of canvas and deciding to leave it unfinished.

Tanzania was not all crabs and crowned cranes on the beach. It was also dodging gunshots aimed at suspicious photographers outside the president's modest palace. It was also bowing to Mwalimu while he was taking a casual stroll on the beach with one single bodyguard. It was also meeting with travelling missionaries who told you stories that they brought back from the countryside to the city. Like the story about the Swahili chief who refused to convert to Christianity because he would then be compelled to keep only one wife. Here, the chief had said, pointing to the wives' houses that surrounded his hut, in what he called a *boma*, he could have a little dinner with each one of his wives, play with her children in turns, and then turn in for the night with his youngest or most favourite wife.

Getting in the sack literally meant getting into a sack in Tanzania. Mzee Rashidi, one of the old field assistants at Gombe, decided to marry a young girl from another village. Mzee Rashidi was fifty-four years old with several grown children. This would be his fourth wedding, and the bride was all of fifteen. The wedding party set off from Gombe for a boat ride across the lake to fetch the bride. As in India, it was considered an ill omen for the groom to see his bride before the actual wedding. This was achieved in an open boat by putting the screaming bride into a gunny sack pulled out from under one of the boat's greasy benches. She howled most unceremoniously while her father, grinning from ear to ear, made light of his burdens to the deafening sound of cymbals and African drums.

Rashidi marries a girl of fifteen

Nights in Tanzania were clear and warm. The stars always seemed to be at touching distance. Indians like us who had never had a clear sighting of the moon from all the city's smog would stay up and bask in the moonlight. We even had annual moon rising parties on the beach on a super moon night when the moon rose closest to the earth. Some beaches get eroded a lot more than others and whole houses sometimes had to be moved back as the sea ravaged compound walls. Where the sea took away from one beach, it gave back to another. Msasani Bay, where Mwalimu Julius Nyerere had built his palace, Derek Bryceson had his two beach houses, and where Jane and I lived, was a little half-saucer of a beach where the sea often built up its sand stock.

True to local tradition, Mwalimu often had hundreds of relatives dropping in on him and staying on for years. Once in, most visitors stayed for as long as they liked. Mwalimu's home was no exception just because he happened to be the president. To accommodate all these guests he had to build another house in the garden so that this increasing tribe of visitors did not interfere with his official routine. In fact, they were much relieved with this new arrangement as it was actually his work that disturbed them. Stories of cruelty and ignorance often floated in from across the palace walls. Stories of dogs being clubbed to death because nervous African guests thought they were possessed by spirits was just one of them. There were stories of guests turning into irate roosters during the day and of angry women turning into jackals and howling all night. The jackals often devoured the roosters.

There was colour in the light of every day. There were days when everything looked blue. The next day it was pale green. The day after, the red glow of the sun would reflect itself on everything there was on the earth. It was as if the sky had chosen to share a deep secret with the waters of the sea. Tall casuarinas held sway over the seascape. The tiny seeds that fell on the sands needed a little bit of moisture to germinate and spring to life another wind-breaking tree. These trees grew easily. They could survive on a little sea water on the beach, on snow-clad mountains, or cultivated gardens; just about anywhere just like me, or so I thought until I came back to India, to the city of Bombay that was to soon become Mumbai.

XI

Five Homes in Goa

'Just so that we knew if that was where we wanted to be.'

When we first came to Goa one wet morning in July 1995, my cousin Mahrukh and I had no plans whatsoever. We had just left the tea gardens of Munnar in Kerala after a motorcycle accident had scared me off riding a bike forever and the prospect of returning to a life in Mumbai seemed daunting. Memories of the communal riots of a year and a half ago had left a deep and indelible scar on our minds, and we were not yet ready to isolate memory from the matter of getting on in this metropolis that is capable of shrugging off any tragedy, any trauma, and any amount of filth with its cracked pavements, leaking drains, and potholes. We took that decision to come to Goa under those compelling circumstances. We had nowhere else to go.

The decision to come to Goa followed a casual invitation from Shirley and Lalit, friends of Elizabeth and Rashid visiting our tea plantation home in Munnar. In the one and a half years that we were in Munnar, Rashid and Liz must have visited us four times. They simply loved it. We loved having them over. Liz and her sister Diane had even driven our little 1984 Maruti 800 down for us all the way from Mumbai while we came by train. They would sometimes bring their friends. Lalit and Shirley were one of those friends. And just when we were wondering what we would do next (the motorcycle accident had left me immobile, Mahrukh was tired of tea plantation life by then and neither of us wanted to go back to Mumbai), Lalit suggested that we take a break in their flat in Goa, a few minutes' walk from the beach at Colva before we actually leave Munnar for good 'just so that we knew if that was where we wanted to be'. I was familiar with Colva (I had stayed there with my colleague and friend Debi Goenka in the GTDC Guest House while on a coastal survey for the Bombay Environmental Action Group) and like any other tourist from Mumbai only knew Goa for its sun, sand, and sea imagery.

There was nothing desperate about our three week stay in Goa. We drove from Munnar, stopping for the night at Kozhikode and were showed around Lalit and Shirley's flat by Bismark 'Biju' Martin who smiled at every naive question we had for him and seemed amused just by the 'two Parsi girls' from Munnar (or Mumbai? How did it matter?) who wanted to come to Goa 'and live'. We awoke to the bells of the church across the street, went for a swim in the sea, walked on the crunchy white sands, and breakfasted in our wet sarongs on scrambled eggs and tea at the small family run shacks on the beach. It was the summer of 1995 and a time when busloads of Indian men would descend on the beach. We were as fascinated by them as they were with us. They would gingerly step on to the sands, small flat briefcases in hand, leather shoes and dark socks, nylon shirts and pants, and a gasp. I guess some of them had never seen the ocean before in their lives. And when they offered ten rupees for the privilege of shaking our hand, we got a taste of what some of the single white women tourists on the beach were facing.

After the constricting life on the tea plantations, where every move was watched and every moment accounted for, the holiday in Goa seemed like heaven. We washed the sand off our feet every evening, hung our swimming things out to dry on the balcony facing the sun, and ate lotus. There was no doubt in our minds that this is where we wanted to be. At the end of the three weeks, however, the pressure started building up. If we were planning to come to Goa and live, we would have to find a place we could rent and also some idea of what we were going to do once we had moved. Although we knew very few people in Goa, both Mahrukh and I had been there on work (as part of an environmental group based in Mumbai that had been asked to survey the coastline of Maharashtra and Goa for me and as a garment inspector in charge of quality control for garments manufactured in Goa for her). Simply put, that was the only connection we had had with this tiny pin head of a state located on the west coast of India. I had no idea of its history then, even less of an idea of its geography and absolutely no intention of starting a movement here for the protection and preservation of its heritage.

The only three people I knew in Goa were Therese and Sarto Almeida and E. R. 'Babush' Godinho. I counted Therese and Sarto amongst my friends. Therese had founded a highly successful school near Margao and was associated with the World Wide Fund for Nature (then the World Wildlife Fund). It was with her that we had made some memorable trips into the interior and 'discovered' temple ruins. It was with Therese that Debi and I had, on an earlier occasion, tracked the shifting of the Shri Mahadeo Temple from Kurdi to Salaulim. The stone by stone shifting of the temple had created quite a stir in heritage circles, and it was with Therese's help that I was able to write an article on it for the *Free Press Journal* in Mumbai.

When Mahrukh and I spoke to them about our decision to come to Goa, Sarto's first reaction was to thump a set of books on Goa in my waiting arms. While Mahrukh worked herself to the bone cleaning Lalit and Shirley's holiday apartment, a welcome change from being waited upon in Munnar by plantation ayah, butler, gardener, and houseboy, I devoured the recorded and published history of a Goa that was far removed from its stereotypical image. It was only later, when I started my own research, that I realised that even that published history of Goa was one version of the real thing. Goa was not a place, really, but an idea, a notion in peoples' heads.

History was one thing but what with all the swimwear and sarong lifestyle, we also needed to visit the beauty salon across the road. That is where we met Annie who, while working on our nails, let slip that her father rented rooms in the village of Betalbatim 'next to Colva'. We decided to go pay her family a visit and also have a look at the rooms. When we went to Betalbatim at the appointed day and time, there was no one home. That was the beginning of a series of 'a different idea of time' in Goa. Anyway, we were too enamoured of Goa then to worry about a whole family that had gone missing. We walked around the village, veered towards the beach, and stopped at a bean field to chat with the couple. Of course, they knew our Annie and also knew that the family would be back in an hour from a village wedding; they also described the guest house that the family rented out to 'foreigners' (and for how much, the thieves), peppering their information desk with stories about this family including why people called Annie's dad Kavllo or Crow.

By the time we walked back to Annie's place and were given a tour of the guest house (available for a hefty Rs 7,000 per month), Kavllo was out of his formal suit and into his one and only pair of shorts that looked to us like it had been riddled with bullet holes. He fired us with a few questions about where we were living while on holiday and told us that he never rented to Indians but considering we were 'girls' and 'known to his daughter Annie' relented and asked us to put down a deposit so he 'would not give it to some other foreigners'. We now had a home to come to after Munnar. We also had friends Therese and Sarto in neighbouring Seraulim village across a few rice fields from Kavllo's Guest House. We also had the ambiguous status of being welcomed as 'foreigners' in our own homeland.

We returned to the tea gardens, handing in our papers, collecting our dues (at salaries of Rs 8,000 a month and hardly anywhere to spend it on our savings were what could be called a nice little nest egg then) and began to get rid of all the trappings of a tea garden life, aiming, quite foolishly, to dispossess ourselves of crockery, cutlery, fine clothes, and tons of books. Luckily for us, my brother Dhunrumi, sister-in-law Yasmin, and their two sons Rustom and Rushad decided to visit us before we left Munnar. Rustom and Rushad took away the books so they would remain in the family. As for the one dinner set that we decided to send to our new home in Goa by truck but all that remained of the twenty-six piece set was close to 2,600 pieces when the set arrived. Kavllo of course was overjoyed. He had been looking for some broken china to bed the new earthing pit in the Guest House garden, and here there was broken china for the asking. Kavllo loved his new guests.

Life in Betalbatim for the next three months began with a routine of freshly tapped toddy for breakfast followed by free beauty treatments, courtesy Annie. We took long walks on the sunlit beach at Betalbatim and ate jackfruit. Life for our landlord revolved around the jackfruit tree. Kavllo had a huge mature tree in the front garden laden with fruit. Our landlord shared this fruit with us with grave generosity. When we could not eat anymore, he would allow some of the fruit to ripen on the tree and then fall to be eaten by the pigs he kept so we could have jackfruit flavoured sausage as a special treat. The old branches of the tree were sawed off once in a while and carved into yellow wood-mite infested cupboards, cabinets, and beds. We used to park our old Maruti 800 under its shade when we were not driving Kavllo around to do his weekly shopping. (He would wrap his own Fiat up in shredded plastic and then ask us to drive him to the market in our car.) So the old jackfruit tree almost always kept us company.

Not that we were in want of company. Our friends and relatives in Mumbai, Mahableshwar, and Nagpur were delighted that we had moved to this 'Mumbai friendly' holiday destination. They would simply pick us up in their cars, grateful that they now had two local guides. With them, we began to explore Goa, veering off the beach belt, and into the lesser known parts, keen on showing our visitors a Goa that was off the beaten track and at the same time wondering what we were going to do for a living once the holiday came to an end. Our savings from Munnar had been put away in Unit Trust 'Units' and were loftily living off its slim interest, too proud to ask my mother in Mumbai for money.

Of all the visitors we had then, the ones that brought a ray of hope into this depressed financial state were Sheila Gandhy and Nari Nullaseth from Mahableshwar. Nari had some land that he owned on the beach in the south Goa village of Agonda that was 'lying unused', and he egged us on to 'do something with it'. We thought it would be a cakewalk. I mean, how difficult would it be to start a tented resort on a south Goa beach that was already popular with the foreign tourists to begin with? After all, we had Biju Martin, also from South Goa (Velim), to help us and we would, as women entrepreneurs, get a bank loan quite easily. We drove off in our little Maruti to see the land, driving as if on a cloud, dreaming that we were running a beach resort already.

Our first lesson in land management in Goa had begun. Nari's land had an invisible boundary with a dozen local villagers crossing the boundary with impunity. The freshwater well that he had been so proud of was in fact not accessible to us. It was to be shared between two Christian neighbours and a Hindu tenant on the property, none of whom were in the Christian mood for sharing. The golden sands that we had expected to see were in fact black with oil slick. The papers that entitled Nari to think that this land was his were actually in the name of some erstwhile 'Maharaja' that no one had even heard of, and we soon realised that no bank would give us a loan of even half a rupee without a collateral or guarantee.

Too desperate to admit defeat, we persisted. We made trips from Betalbatim to the taluk offices of South Goa in Chavdi, seeking advice from ill-humoured government officials (who I think were too bemused at our naiveté to take us seriously but who nonetheless gave us tips on how to order tank loads of water, load them on to the backs of trucks, and store them on the beach and how to import chemical toilets from a company in the UK), a distance of about twenty-two kilometres each way with scarcely enough money to stop for lunch en route even less for petrol for the Maruti.

At the end of the eighth trip to the Chavdi offices, with no end in sight, I decided to seek the advice of an old friend in the Town & Country Planning Office in Panaji. Although I had always met 'Babush' E. R. Godinho in an official capacity in the past, 'Babush' had always been courteous and warm and forthcoming. Maharukh and I walked into his office one morning and coyly shared our dream of running a resort at this 'free land' that had fallen into our laps at Agonda. 'Babush' must have spent not more than a minute listening to our grand plans and promptly pricked our bubble. 'If there is no water on this land, forget it. Drop the plan.' The investment needed just to get water tanks on the land was more than the savings we had in the bank. We did not need any further persuasion. Several hundred rupees lighter, we were back in Betalbatim and began our money worries seriously.

Life, however, was not without its funny moments. We had arrived in the rains, and Kavllo had his car shrouded in bits and pieces of flimsy plastic to shield his car from the downpour. After the rain, we would often watch him take all the plastic bits off the car and then take his 'shot to bits' shorts off and wipe the car dry. When he was quite satisfied that his old Fiat was now drip dry, he would wring the shorts and then put them back on. There was also the primary school incident, which to me was a great example of a Goan voice. Kavllo's wife taught at the village primary school every morning. One morning, I could see the little ones in their classes waiting for their teacher. I was wondering if she was unwell and had not gone to the school. 'Why, Auntie, no school today?' I asked. 'Oh, I washed my hair today no? So I'm not going to school. I might catch cold' was her reply.

Then there was the family feud over an egg. Annie had warned us not to speak to her uncle and aunt who lived next door. The two families shared water from the family-owned well but had not spoken to each other in decades. 'But this is your dad's brother!' I protested. 'What is the fight about anyway?' 'It seems one of their hens came into our compound and laid an egg. So we took the egg, right? They say it's their hen so we should have given them the egg. But it was in our compound, so it's ours!' The two brothers and their families had not spoken to each other over one single egg.

And then there was the 'never' on a Sunday Lament. Annie would refuse to go to church on Sunday (or any other day) for some reason. We would often question her about it and receive evasive replies. The village church was not more than a few minutes' walk from the house, and there would be a long line of women, young and old, dressed to the gills (huge plastic flowers topping flowery flouncy gowns) at six in the morning on their way to Sunday Mass that Annie could, we were sure, easily join. After we had done talking to her, it was the turn of the village priest. He would come on his motorcycle on Monday morning and ask in the most solicitous tone if Annie had been ill on Sunday. 'Why not go for Mass instead of having the priest visit every Monday?' we asked. An exasperated Annie then spilled the beans. 'Do I have a new dress to wear every Sunday? How can I go for Mass?' she cried.

There was also the 'you should have died episode'. Our rental at Kavllo's Guest House in Betalbatim was drawing to a close and we had been house hunting with Biju Martin in and around his home at Velim further south. All of a sudden, we got hit by a storm. There was thunder, lightning, and lots of rain, and we could not get home for hours. When we did get to Betalbatim, however, we were greeted by a neighbour who lived at the top of the road with a rather startling, '*Oye*, you girls are here, eh? You should have *died* men!' The storm had apparently been very focussed. A lightning bolt had struck one neighbour's house, destroying her television set, bounced off a light bulb in the veranda that was our usual perch in the guest house, and then blown the ancient refrigerator at Kavllo's. What the neighbour at the top of the road no doubt meant was that had we been sitting at our usual spots in the veranda we might have been at the receiving end of the lightning strike.

Perhaps the storm was a sign from heaven, and it really was time to leave Kavllo's Guest House. We could barely afford the Rs 7,000 rent let alone Kavllo's expectation of Rs 15,000 per month in the tourist season that was fast approaching. With Biju's efforts (after several trials and errors), we finally found a terrace room (what people in the north of India would call a *barsaati*) with Maria Arcanja in what was the shortest address we had ever lived in. Behind Pinto Bar, Varca. It was a multi-functional room that had been designed and built by Maria Arcanja's uncle for himself. A bed and a desk, a chair, two deck chairs, and a coffee table comprised all the room's furniture. Large picture windows all around the room, however, gave us a view of the grounds beyond the house and the *pot pourri* of plants in Maria's garden. We also had a clear view of the front gate and all the happenings in the neighbourhood, sometimes our only entertainment. We had to dip into our meagre savings (some more dues had arrived in the bank account from Tata Tea Ltd. by then) to buy a washing machine and a fridge (both Videocon as that was the only brand our budget would allow) leaving us with as little as Rs 1,500 to live on for the whole month after paying Maria Arcanja her modest rent.

It would have been impossible to live on as little as that at today's prices, but in October 1994 one could stretch it. Or rather, we did. We used to buy one packet of milk (half a litre) and then stretch it over two days. We bought the cheapest rice there was at Rs 10 a kilo. We ate watery *dhal* and went shopping to Margao (a distance of eight kilometre one way) for greens once a week and did all our own housework as there was no question of paying for a maid. Our landlady lived with her two sons, Ludio and Gracio, and a man servant José, Portuguese for Joseph (later my inspiration for the short story Dona Argentina). Ludio was already in high school when we lived with them, but Gracio, in kindergarten, soon took to running up the stairs after school especially when his mother and José took to watching *Shanti* on afternoon television.

Television was not the only thing that Gracio wanted to escape from. He hated curry and rice, a staple at the ground floor household. He began to enjoy our simple *dhal* and rice, chapattis, and vegetables and was fascinated by the fact that we did not eat at a dining table but simply pulled two deck chairs and leaned over a coffee table over steel *thalis*. Gracio had been a 'poor eater' until then, and Maria Arcanja was so grateful that her son was 'eating well' that she began to send us little bits and pieces of food from her table. I think that she saw our frugal lifestyle and decided to help us out while being tactful about it.

Besides being a kind, loving, and generous human being, Maria was also an environmentalist without even knowing it. Everything got recycled in the house, nothing was wasted. The pigs she kept ate the leftovers and green waste, the chickens ate up the skins from the kitchen, the dogs and cats polished off all the animal bones and skins clean, and whatever little paper waste there was would be used to start the evening fires. Maria also used a lot of home remedies to cure us of our coughs, colds, and skin irritations. Her whole garden was filled with *tulsi,* sacred basil from which she would concoct potions for coughs and colds. Raw guavas were given to us when we had sore throats or upset stomachs, and in the rains, José and she would scour the open lands around the house for wild plants that were good to eat.

Although we had decided to live on our own and have 'very little to do with families', Mahrukh's two sisters and only brother did not give up on us. Whenever they'd visit, they would bring armloads of gifts (perfumes, clothes, chocolates) which we almost never had any use for. Our evening outings were restricted to long walks in the village up to the Varca beach. So we would unwrap the gifts carefully, rewrap them in the same wrapping papers, and store them away safely to give away 'just in case we got invited someplace'. We saved on buying gifts that way because buying things on our budget was simply out of the question. I did bring back little gifts for Mahrukh on my way back from the grocery stores in the village *tinto* though. I would pick up fallen leaves with pretty patterns, sometimes the big fleshy flowers of the silk cotton trees, curls of sweet smelling green tamarind that the three-banded chipmunks had dropped on their way up and down the old tamarind trees.

Fortunately, our poor economic status meant nothing to our fellow villagers. We got invited to all the 'functions' in the village. Through Maria Arcanja and her relatives and friends, we began to meet other people. Friends from Mumbai would often drop by and take us out for dinner where we met other Goans who, in turn, would invite us over for birthdays and weddings. It was while living with Maria Arcanja that we understood the Goan fetish for celebrating a birthday. Birthdays had always been a 'cake and candles' affair during our growing up years, but once we had passed that stage, we simply went out to a restaurant for dinner on our birthdays or spent the day quietly by ourselves.

A Goan birthday celebration is something else. The house gets a thorough cleaning, paper and tinsel decorations are put up, the parish priest often drops by to bless the birthday boy or girl, and almost all the neighbours and friends file into the house with a gift. All the chairs in the house are lined up with their backs to the wall with the centre of the room left vacant and you take a chair in near complete silence. You are given a plate of food that you consume without any space for conversation in between mouthfuls. The birthday girl or boy is then escorted to the guests that are older (like Ludio was escorted to us), and we are expected to shower the birthday celebrant with all sorts of advice and severity of counsel. 'Ludio, now you know you have not done very well at school this year. You must try harder, child, and especially in your Hindi lessons, and so on.' What's more, you got invited only once to a birthday celebration. Once invited, you were supposed to make a note in your diary and make it a point to come and wish the birthday girl or boy the following year. And heaven help you if you forget. You can brace yourself to hear any accusation except the most severe one of all, 'You forgot my birthday!'

It was the same with funerals. You were informed of someone's passing away, and then you were expected to make a note of the date so that you could be present in the church at the month's mind (most often a month after the funeral but not necessarily so) and also for the first death anniversary which is sometimes as big an affair as the funeral itself. I still remember how Maria and José would flick open the *Navhind Times* and turn to the page where the obituaries were to ask each other, 'Who went today?' Literally, '*Kaun melo?*' roughly translated as who died? If there was a funeral in the village, they would both have to reschedule their day.

Speaking of funerals, we were in for a shock one morning. We had just woken up and I had stepped out of our room and walked through the little passage to get to our pocket-sized kitchen when I looked to my right and on to the terrace. I thought I was imagining things. One quarter of the terrace will filled with what looked like human bones. Mahrukh couldn't believe her eyes. Was our sweet-tempered landlady a closet murderer? Maria walked up the stairs, smiling, just then. 'Oh, that's my uncle', she said quite cheerfully. We just stood there and gaped. What we did not know then was that because of the paucity of available gravesites in church yards, bodies are often exhumed after three years or so, and the bones of the deceased loved ones handed over to the next of kin. Maria's uncle had obviously been still wet from the grave and was being laid out on the terrace to dry.

Years later, one of our friends from Mumbai went to inspect a heritage house with a view to buying it and got a shock in more or less the same way. She opened the built-in wall cupboard in the crumbling dining room and came face to face with a human skeleton. Keeping better composure than we did, she turned to the house owner only to be told that that was 'only my uncle'. So when we walked into a faux antique showroom at Varca one day with some visiting friends from Mumbai we were quite nonchalant when we saw human bones displayed in the faux antique glass case embedded in the showroom wall. I think we won a few notches as local guides that afternoon with our 'city bumpkin' Mumbai friends.

Meanwhile, money worries were still mounting. Apart from the Munnar savings that we had instinctively invested in the highly popular Unit Trust of India scheme US-64 (it had a nice ring to it. We knew nothing about investing money wisely) and 'living off the interest', we had no other source of income. We had tightened our belts till they could be tightened no further and there were also the weekly phone calls that we had to make to our families to let them know we were doing fine and did not need any help. After years of having my picture in the papers and being quoted for my heritage preservation campaigns in Mumbai, I craved a life of anonymity, away from the newspapers. Ironically, all I had to start over here in Goa was my portfolio with its collection of articles written by me. Our work experience in Munnar counted for nothing.

I soon realised that my work experience in Mumbai also counted for next to nothing. Maria Arcanja generously loaned us the newspapers every morning, and one day I picked up courage and called the editor of the *Navhind Times*. Arun Sinha was either bored or curious that morning because he asked me to come over to his office. I did not want to meet him with a trawl of old articles so I got introductions into three heritage houses and did what I call 'Personality Profiles' on these three homes and their owners. I picked up my portfolio and the articles and took an inter-city bus to Panaji and a city bus to the newspapers office where I met Arun and his secretary Julie in what was the beginning of a long and stable friendship.

Arun said that he was interested and said he would send a photographer from the newspaper to take some pictures for the articles. I did not have a camera. I was ecstatic until he told me that the papers in Goa did not pay very well if anything at all. My heart sank, but I remembered Therese's sound words of advice. 'Get a foothold, and if that is not possible, get a toe hold'. I had my toe hold in the *Navhind Times* with the princely promise of Rs 250 per article. Anyways, photographer Daryl Andrade turned up a few days later, and I found myself on the back of his scooter (my legs bowed for a week after the rides) showing him the three houses that I had written about, expecting in my characteristic naive fashion that this would trigger off a whole series of regular features on the beautiful houses of Goa.

It did not quite turn out that way. Arun had a second look at the articles, saw the pictures that Daryl had taken such pains over, and scowled, 'Why did you choose to write about these particular houses?' I had no answer. It took me years to understand that these houses were seen as *bhatkar*, landlord houses, and the Goan *bhatkar* was not the best loved landlord in the world. It took me years to understand the nuances of the Brahmin, Chardos, and Shudra caste houses that made up the gamut of domestic architecture in Goa. It would take me a lifetime to understand what divided Catholic houses from Hindu homes. It has taken a lot of studying 'the book of human nature' in Goa to come to the easy and reckless conclusion that Goan society is perhaps the most caste-ridden, bigoted, caste-prejudiced, xenophobic, and complex society in the country. Let's just say that I have not watched any other community as closely as the Goan.

The first thing a Goan will ask you after he or she knows your name is 'Where are you coming from?' Now this is not an innocent question. It is loaded with several questions all rolled into one. Your Goan host is also asking you what village you come from, what *vaddo* in the village, who your grandparents were, who your parents, and so on, thereby determining to what caste and social strata you belong. In fact, many old timers will not even go further after they have fired the first question. Your answer to the first will give them all the other answers that will put you in that tight social niche from which there is no escape, either for you or for them.

If you're a Hindu, they will be able to pin point your caste, sub-caste, *gotra*, clan, family, and so on with a little gossip and scandal thrown in for good measure. If you are a Catholic, then you can be sure they will know your family down to the smallest root, including what your caste and last name was before your ancestors converted to Christianity. Even if you are a Catholic, your root caste is really important, and most Christians in Goa know if they were once Shudra, Chardo (Kshatriya), or Brahmin. Without a doubt, this determines whether you can be admitted into a Goan home by the front door or should be let in by the back gate.

With my ability to 'read' a house like you read a book, I could study the social life of a community by just looking at their houses. We walked around the villages of Varca and Orlim a lot in those days. We saw a lot of houses, old *bhatkar* mansions and new concrete Gulf-style boxes. Typically, the large Brahmin and Chardo mansions had a high plinth, stone benches, or seats on either side of the stairs as you climbed, a *balcão*, patio, and then a highly ornate entrance doorway. There were often ornamented windows that faced the road and plain unornamented ones that were off the road and faced the mansion's own backyard or the village commons.

**A high plinth, stone benches and seating usually
make up the entrance to a Goan house**

To me, it was as plain as day. Newly converted Goans were compelled to display their wealth and their newfound religion through their houses. They decorated the windows that faced the road and thereby made an impression on passers-by, neighbours, and the village priests. A high plinth in the front made stairs mandatory. Stairs gave the added advantage of adding posture, prestige and dignity to an otherwise ordinary family home. What a grand impression you made when you dressed for church on a Sunday morning and descended a wide staircase with beautifully moulded stone railings while lesser mortals simply walked out of their doors.

Bhatkars were also the moneylenders of the village. Borrowers and supplicants must feel really small and humble walking up those stairs or waiting for the *bhatkar* to come out of the house seated on the edge of a stone seat at the foot of the stairs. Regulars who visited the house, like the fishmonger, the *puder,* breadman would have easy access to the house by the back gate. The rear ends of these homes were often built flush with the lie of the land. In fact, these grand Goan homes are like two houses built to look like one. The first half has a grand stairway, a *balcão,* an *entrada,* and two reception rooms on either side of the *entrada* followed by a large dining room, sometimes a courtyard that functions as the lung of this rather stifling arrangement and then the actual living spaces like the bedrooms, kitchen, stores, and firewood sheds.

What interested me is that the frontal spaces are like display showcases. Crammed with objects of art, mirrors, vases, curios, china, articulate rosewood furniture and white cement floors that were prepared for dancing, the reception rooms were self-consciously designed for formal receptions, parties, and funeral wakes. The real house, where the family actually lived was at the rear. This area had floors plastered with cow dung paste, pots and pans and baskets lined up on bamboo rafts over the ceilings, onions, chillies, and strings of garlic hanging over wood-fired stoves and a few functional articles of clothing, and cooking lying around higgledy-piggledy all over this spatial arrangement. While the front was an epitome of strict order and an air of pretentiousness that was almost painful, the back was a comfort zone of tradition, habit, and unpretentiousness.

So now we began to see why, when we went to someone's house in the village, they would appear warm and forthcoming and yet never invite us in. The Goan *balcão* was a screening device. You trudged up the stairs of the grand mansion; you were invited to sit on the *sopos,* the benches in the *balcão,* while your hosts grilled you and ratified your ancestry. When you passed muster, you graduated to being invited inside the house, never kept hanging and waiting in the *entrada,* the entrance hall. Once you were accepted, you were in and that was it. It was much later that I learnt that Goans were adept at picking out all your ancestors and slotting your lineage within seconds of knowing your name.

We were a source of frustration. On the one hand, we were two strangers from Bombay with strange names and no lineage that anyone could trace. On the other hand, 'the two Parsi girls' was almost like a password to social acceptance. I cannot remember the number of times that we heard, 'Oh, my uncle worked on the ships and he had many Parsi friends' or 'I worked in the Docks and I had many Parsi friends'. Much later, when Mum and I were on speaking terms again she would say, 'Oh, Goans and Parsis have always been close. After all, we eat the same curry'.

Speaking to strangers and talking to the neighbours in Varca was all very well, but there was still the burning issue of staying alive. I went to Arun once again and asked him for more work. He asked me if I would care to review the few books that were being tossed into the *Navhind Times*. I grabbed the books, most of which were the 'self-help' types and for which I received a paltry Rs 150. Soon the *Gomantak Times*, the *Herald*, and the *Goa Today* began to take notice. I began to do a regular column for the *Gomantak* on Nature, with Mahrukh pitching in with illustrations and the odd article for the *Goa Today*. That beefed up our income by another Rs. 250 or so a week. Clearly, something more had to be done. We were not going to be able to pay the grocery bills. In fact, they were not enough to cover the bus fare to Panaji or even the odd phone calls that I had to make to the newspaper editors.

I recall a particularly desperate phone call to Arun asking him if I could do any kind of regular writing for his newspaper. He must have sensed the desperation in my voice because he said to me, 'We are very short of good fiction. If you can write a short story, I will carry it'. I had never written a short story in my life but faced with the only choice of that or nothing, I went home and sat at my desk, wondering where and how to begin. I do not know what made me think of this man that had broken a sort of world record and lived with snakes in a cage. I wrote the story 'Snakeman'.

Arun loved it. He carried it in the Sunday papers and passed me a letter from Homi Bhabha Fellow and Fulbright Scholar Manohar Shetty, telling me that he had read the story, liked it, and asking me if 'I was a Goan'. I wrote back and we met up at his home in Dona Paula near Panaji that he shared with his beautiful wife Devika and two lovely daughters. Manohar was editing an anthology of Goan short fiction (later published by Penguin titled *Ferry Crossing*) and he needed someone to read the short stories written in Marathi. I offered to read the stories for him, pick the ones that were good enough to be included in the anthology, and translated these into English. Manohar said he was on a very meagre grant from the Homi Bhabha Fellowship Council and the only thing he could give me was the postage stamps for me to be able to post the translated material to him. In other words, I translated over fifty stories from Marathi to English for Manohar to read and got paid in postage stamps. Of course, Manohar made up for it later by showing me how to apply for a Homi Bhabha Fellowship.

Never having paid much attention to fiction in the past, here I was writing short stories for the local paper and translating from the Marathi into the English for an anthology to be published by Penguin. But besides earning a name for myself through this work, there were very few pickings. I was too busy to worry about where life was taking us to see what we were really doing.

However, life comes in strange packages. Mine came in the form of a book whose title I just cannot remember today. It was a book edited by a Goan author named Mario Cabral é Sá that was supposed to bring investors into Goa. Several people I got to know later and had known in Bombay in the past (like the late Bal Mundkur who had also moved to Goa from Mumbai in the same year that we had) had written articles in the book. I carried the package home and sat down to write the review, never once realising that I was expected to sing praises of this book that was sponsored by a leading Goan industrialist and mine owner. I did an honest review. I lambasted the book, poking holes in every article, critical of all the phrases that were leading up to Goa as an investor's paradise. I still remember Arun's face when he read the review across the desk. 'Are you sure you want to say this?' he asked. Naive about how things worked in Goa and how the system of mutual back scratching was so well-entrenched, I made the fatal error of standing my ground and saying, 'Yes'.

The review got printed in the *Navhind Times* and Mario Cabral stormed into the editor's office. 'Who is this girl and who does she think she is?' being the general vein of the one-sided conversation. This storming session triggered off a whole series of events that I was unaware of then and that would have some long-lasting repercussions. Mario had not only stormed the editor's office, he went to town on this. As a result, every editor in Goa got to know about this 'upstart from Bombay'. 'Babush' Godinho must have heard and so did architect Gerard da Cunha who had a 'no love lost' kind of relationship with Mario over some old bone that nobody even remembered.

Unknown to me, people had begun to take sides. There was the 'anti-upstart' faction, and there was the 'who is this brave girl?' faction. No one apparently had challenged Mario's legendary authority over the subject of Goa up until now. No one else was an expert on Konkani, Marathi, Portuguese, English, and Goa until today. He was author, authority, and ability all rolled into one, and he had declared me his enemy publicly. I was to shiver in my boots and the one to keep me abreast of all the furore was my poor friend 'Babush'. Mario began to hound me after that. He was critical of everything I wrote, every word I spoke, and every presentation I was to give later during my stay in 'his state'. I felt then as I do now that many people simply read my writing (and his letter to the editor that would invariably follow) or came to my talks simply to watch the fun. Of all the things that I was in any doubt of in Goa, one thing was certain: Goa and Goans loved a good fight.

'Babush' knew that we were struggling to survive. I received a message through him from architect Gerard da Cunha in North Goa. Gerard was planning a book on the houses of Goa and wondered if I would be interested in meeting him. I remember taking the car out that afternoon thinking I would soon have the money for petrol. I met with the architect in his office, a rented heritage house in Sangolda on CHOGM road, and his gentle mannerism put me at ease instantly. Gerard showed me an article he had written on the house he had designed and built for businessman Jimmy Guzder. The house was a real cliff hanger, overlooking the Aguada Jail on one side and the ocean on the other and had created quite a sensation in Goa. Gerard sat me down and asked me to read the article. I read it word by word and looked at him. He then said, 'I want to do a book on the houses of Goa, but I don't have the time. I am looking for someone who can write like I would'. I did not know then that what he was actually asking me to do was ghost-write his book on Goan houses.

Gerard's original idea was to do a kind of catalogue on the houses of Goa. The book would have, he explained, an inventory of the various styles of windows, doors, roofs, wall ornamentation, and so on. Most of the work for the book had already been done by his senior architect Annabel Mascarenhas, and all I had to do was 'put it together'. Annabel handed me a whole pile of books that she said would fill me in on the research. I carried the pile back to the car, planning to put a completely different proposal before them. 'Let me get back to you with an outline for a book on the houses of Goa. If you don't like my outline, you pay me Rs 5,000 for my effort and we call it quits. If you like my outline and 'chapterization' for the book, then you pay me nothing, but we go ahead with the work on a separate set of terms.' Looking back, I really do not know how I had the nerve to put such a proposal before him.

I went back to Varca with Mahrukh, waiting to hear 'if I had got the job'. From her point of view, I hadn't. While I worked on the outline, she began to scan the papers for job opportunities that might come her way. One morning, she rushed in with the *Navhind Times* and showed me an advertisement, inviting applications for a Quality Control Manager at the Wrangler Jeans factory in distant Bicholim. Not knowing if the outline idea would succeed with Gerard and how much money it would bring in, I encouraged her to call the number in the ad, half-imagining that the ad was just a mandatory formality and the place had already been filled in by someone on the inside. I was wrong. I took her to Bicholim for the interview, and she came back from the industrial estate smiling. We now had a job!

Wrangler had given us a week. We began to look for houses to rent in the town, but instead of a house on rent, we were faced with suspicion, sarcasm, and a thorny bouquet of Mumbai rent rates for some rather sorry spaces. Everyone we knew began to give us a hand, including our generous landlady Maria Arcanja. My respect for her went up a few notches when she was asked if we were Hindu or Christian by a potential landlady in North Goa. 'How does it matter?' she said. 'They are human beings.' What was also interesting to us was the standard question, 'Do you salt your rice before it goes into the pot or after?' That question always puzzled me until years later I was given the answer by a professor at the Goa University. The wealthy in Goa (and therefore by virtue the upper classes) apparently used copper pots for cooking their rice. In order to avoid the salt from reacting with the copper, they would not add salt to the rice in the pot. The poor on the other hand, cooked in clay pots, and could add salt to the rice before it was cooked. The answer to the question then was simply a roundabout way for a new landlady to determine to which class we belonged.

In between all the house hunting and the trauma of leaving little Gracio, Arcanja's son, of whom we had grown very fond, there were what I call Varca moments. There was the incident of a very drunk neighbour clanging the gate in the middle of the night determined to ask Arcanja for a refill. When she refused, he began to get abusive, and she called the local police station. A sleepy policeman answered the phone and offered to come and look into the matter except that they had no official transport. Maria Arcanja, equally determined not to let the matter go offered to send her own car. José took off in the little yellow Fiat to fetch the policemen from the village station. By now, with all the excitement and the shouting, Maria Arcanja's dogs were in frenzy. So when the policemen arrived, the dogs, familiar with the neighbour but not with the policemen, decided to do their own bit to help the family. They attacked the policemen.

We would miss Varca and living with Maria Arcanja, Gracio, Ludio, and José. We would miss the carnival of the village. Where else in the world would the *Anopheles* mosquito be the theme for a week of fun and fantasy? Where else in the world would a Volkswagen Beetle be covered in brown paint and dressed up as a mosquito? Where else in the world would a *bhatkar*, landlord force his *mundkar*, tenant to stay in his car for forty-eight hours while the car was being covered with brown sacking and paint so the *mundkar* could drive it in the parade the next day? Obviously, the annual carnival did not share legal space with labour laws or the rights of the peasants.

We did not know what the future would hold for us. It was as if we would be on our own for the first time. Over the past few months, we had not just shared our living quarters with our landlady, we had shared our lives. We had admired her 'zero garbage' lifestyle where all the vegetable waste went to the pigs she kept, all the bones went to the dogs and cats, and whatever was left over from the dogs, cats and pigs went to the chickens. Maria had an incinerator for our Mumbai-style waste (mostly paper), and José happily used a piggy toilet. There were people in and out of her home. She even had guests from England who landed up every few months, took showers by the well in the backyard, and hung their towels out on the kitchen chairs. Everyone in the village called them 'the hippies' long after the whole hippie cult in Goa had faded away. I am quite certain they did have proper English names.

It was while we were at Varca that we saw, for the first time ever, how a sow made a nest from branches and twigs three times her own size and actually prepared her delivery room before giving birth to eight little piglets. When the piglets had grown to the right size, Maria and José would castrate them with a kitchen knife without any anaesthetic so they would grow 'nice and fat and not waste their wealth on other things'. It's a wonder those poor little pigs did not bleed to death. Or did they? Only *sorpotel* could tell.

Mahrukh's future colleagues at Wranglers were also trying to help us find a place. They had recommended a lovely little house right outside Bicholim where the industrial estate was, and we scooted off to see it and meet the landlord. The house stood in the middle of arecanut and coconut palms. A lovely little brook played with the morning sunshine by the side of the house. The landlord lived on the ground floor with his family and was willing to let us rent the upstairs. We just had to negotiate the price except that the price was not negotiable. He wanted Rs 7,000 every month. Mahrukh was to bring home a pay packet of Rs 8,000. That would leave us with less spending money than what we had when we were not working.

I cannot remember how we finally landed up in the flat in Mapusa, twenty-two kilometres away from her workplace, but we were to spend three and a half years there, and they would be the happiest days of our lives in Goa. Now you wouldn't think that a small market town like Mapusa would be attractive in anyway, but Mapusa offered vibrancy, vigour, and neighbours like nowhere else we had been before. What was the most attractive thing about the town was that it was affordable. We would walk down to the Friday Market once a week, come back loaded with fish, fruit, and vegetables we could barely carry, feast over the weekend, and make jams, *murabbas* and preserves with the fruit that we had bought cheaply.

If there was one thing that was missing in our new home, it was furniture. We had always rented places that included furniture, and this flat came with none. All we had was a cane shoe rack that Mahrukh had picked up from one of her trips to Mumbai. Well, the shoe rack was a start we consoled ourselves. Things would soon fall into place. My brother and his family visited us on their short holiday to Goa and were horrified at the way we were living. They were, of course, comparing our luxury tea garden bungalow in Munnar with the fifty-square metres minimalistic existence that my friend Parimal Gandhi had earlier described as 'moving down in life'. My brother Dhunrumi could not help himself. He asked us to buy a sofa for the living room right away, offering to give it to us as a gift. We were both so deeply touched. I shall never forget the feeling of that first purchase. We had seen a cane three-piece sofa on one of our trips at Gurim on the outskirts of Mapusa for about that much and ordered it at 'DK's'.

If 'DK' sounded like a furniture boutique on a beach, you'd be completely off your rocker. It was just an acronym of Dyaneshwar Kamlakar whose only passion in life was to make cane furniture, play cricket, and be captain of the team he had started up in the village. To follow up on your order, you had to go to the temple first and see if the team was at play in the temple grounds, lure 'DK' out of the heat of the game with promises of bringing more 'Bombay people' to have a look at his cane furniture. All the money he made went into the buying of cricket equipment for the village team.

Soon our cricket crazy supplier became a regular guest at the flat. We were rich enough to buy the three piece sofa with my brother's generous grant and bought our own twin beds soon after that. With 'DK', you did not have to worry about transport and delivery. He would come in the blazing Goan afternoon in a three wheeler tempo, bind the furniture with nylon ropes, and then come into the house grinning from ear to ear. He would then haul the beds into the house through our tiny balcony, free them of their ropes, and arrange them in our bedroom. If we offered him a portion of our lunch, he would turn up his nose in disgust but politely tell us he had to go home to eat. Our everyday fare of *rajma* and rice must have looked like pig's swill in comparison with his mother's *xitt kodi.*

It was those days in Mapusa that taught us that there were very few Goans who could eat anything but their beloved rice and fish curry. It was also those Mapusa days that showed us how everyone connected in Goa in rather strange and uncanny ways. 'DK', for example, would tell us how he would go and take a swim in a luxury private swimming pool overlooking the Aguada beach when the owner of the villa was away in Bombay. The caretaker of the luxury villa was a friend of his, and he had, over the years, developed a regular arrangement to swim. It did not take us very long to guess that the villa he was referring to was owned by businessman Jimmy Guzder, the very villa that had been designed and built by architect Gerard da Cunha and the subject of the magazine article Gerard had shown me.

Living in Mapusa brought us optimism and a great sense of security. Mahrukh was commuting twenty-two kilometres each way in our Maruti 800, and Gerard had loved my proposal for the book even though it meant that the catalogue idea that he and Annabel had worked on would have to be tossed out completely. I began working on the book in earnest, taking a bus to the Government of Goa Archives in Panaji to do my research and meet with fellow researcher Fr. Nascimento Mascarenhas who proved to be an invaluable friend and guide throughout the rest of my stay, cooking simple dinners, cleaning our third floor flat in between, and working on my manual typewriter at night.

Good things began to happen. Gerard placed an offer of Rs 50,000 for writing the text for the book. I met one of my finest friends in Rukshana Sarosh, the designer for the book and her lovely family, and I began to make amends with my own family in Mumbai. There was money in the house to make weekly phone calls to my parents and a monthly call to my sister in the US. Mobiles were a thing of the future and neither Mahrukh nor I had dreams of ever owning a phone. We were doing so well then that when Gomantak Times (now GT) refused to pay more than Rs 200 for the Sunday column that I was doing for them (including an illustration done by Mahrukh) we actually put a stop to the weekly contribution.

I began to get in touch with friends in Mumbai, old colleagues in the Indian Heritage Society (Bombay Chapter) and the Indian National Trust for Art and Cultural Heritage better known as INTACH. My social networking in Goa also improved by leaps and bounds, thanks to Rukshana's dad Feroze (incidentally a collector of the largest private collection of still and movie cameras in the world) who had made it his life's mission to bring us out of our shell. He would come over on a weekend and drag Mahrukh out to the plant nurseries on the outskirts of town to help him pick up plants for his garden in Candolim. Cancer stole him from all of us years later and neither his family nor his friends have ever recovered from this irreparable loss.

Most people don't know this, but it takes a very long time to recover from a state of penury. It is not as if one day you did not have money and the next day you do and all is well. It took us six to eight months to recover from the poor state we had been in. Eating poorly and as and when neighbours had sent us food had done some damage to our health. 'So did you just go on a diet?' my friend Cyrus Guzder had asked once jokingly when we met him at the Taj Aguada Holiday Village. In fact, I said to him, one had to be rich to go on a diet. When you were poor, you just ate what you could when you could, and it was not always food that was healthy. You had to make do with food that was cheap, and that meant your diet was mostly potatoes, cheap rice, and bread that the local *puder* brought to you on his rounds every morning and evening.

Mahrukh was blessed with a body that never succumbed to fat, but I was a victim of unhealthy eating. Little did Cyrus know that the voluminous dress that I was wearing the day we went to see him and his wife Manek at the Taj had burst a front button because it was too tight and that we had stopped at the roadside tea lady outside the Aguada Fort to ask if she had a safety pin. Goa being Goa, she did better than that. She had a little box by the side of her stove and matches and things, and the little box had a small reel of sewing thread and an enormous needle. As the afternoon breeze blew the dress around, Mahrukh stood guard while the tea lady's little box saved the day.

Mapusa, Mahrukh's job at Wrangler, and my book writing project had given us the independence of renting our own flat, driving our own car, and choosing our own neighbours. We had jobs, friends, and furniture. We now had a life. However, just like our bodies had taken a toll during the lean period, we had suffered earlier; our little Maruti too was showing signs of age and deprivation. Every time we took the car out, it would get stuck with one minor repair or another. Japanese on the outside, the little Maruti 800 was definitely Indian on the inside. She would cough and splutter and get hot under the bonnet but never once did she let us down on the road. She would wait for us to arrive at the house before one or the other part collapsed.

The location of the flat did not help matters either. Mapusa, the main town, is flat but the suburb we were in, Khorlim, is a steep hill that really takes the Mickey out of you and leads you up to the garden village of Assagao. As luck would have it, Gangadhar Apartments was at the top of the highest point in Khorlim and our flat the topmost floor, at the highest part of the building. We had to park the car at the foot of the apartment. Even carrying groceries up to the flat from the car left us breathless.

Our location, however, had its own set of joyful offerings. A pair of sunbirds twittered in and out of the house from the trees that almost touched our windows and a fungoid frog had made our kitchen his permanent refuge. We had a name for him too, although he never let us know he knew it. We used to call him PC, short for Prince Charming. On weekends, we often took a small picnic lunch and headed out to the beach or drove down to Calangute for an early breakfast at Infantaria Bakery, working hard at playing the 'girls from Bombay' as the Mhapshekars called us behind our backs.

However, all was not well in paradise. Some of Bombay's problems had obviously followed us here as well. The building, perched on top of a steep hill, was so located as to not get more than a few drops of water from the city's supply. There was a sump at the bottom of the building from which overhead tanks were supposed to fill and then run through taps and showers into every flat. Water pressure being what it was it, just ran out of steam when it reached our building, clogged our pipes, and air-locked every tap and faucet. On most days, we had to fill buckets at the sump (drawing water from the sump as if it were a village tank) and haul the buckets up to the flat, three flights up and then three flights down again.

Angry and exhausted from the effort, we confronted the builder and his young son one afternoon only to get a shocking reply from him. 'Oh, we did not expect anyone to come and actually live in this place.' They had, in fact, not given a single thought to a regular water supply to the building they had designed and built. Tired of the water problem as we were, the crisis brought us all closer. Our neighbours were helpful and caring and never once did we get a feeling that we were in the middle of a contest. When things got really bad, Ashok Amre and his wife Anita who lived in a modest-sized house next to our apartment block would let us draw water from their perennial well.

Ashok and his son Mohan were both taxi drivers by profession. Ashok's wife Anita was an excellent cook, and during our drought days, she would often send us food so we did not have to cook. We used to park our Maruti

800 behind Ashok's black-and-yellow taxi, praying every night that the brakes on his battered old warhorse were secure. Well, obviously we had not prayed hard enough. As it so happened, Gerard had come over to the flat one morning, looking for some reference books and had parked in the only spot available on the slope. When he left the flat to go back to his car, he found Ashok's car awkwardly looping over his. What followed was something like this: Ashok comes out of his house in his khaki shorts and ragged vest. '*Kitey,*' what's this? Ashok asks Gerard. Gerard is also in his trademark shorts, only less ragged. '*Kitey?*' he answers. After a couple of '*Kiteys*' going backwards and forwards between Ashok and Gerard, everybody soon realises that Gerard's Konkani language skills are rather limited.

Working on the book on the houses of Goa was a memorable experience. It was a first timer for each one of us. Gerard had never been a publisher before; Rukshana had never designed a book; it was Ashok Koshy's first illustrated book assignment, and my first attempt at writing a book. In theory, it should not have worked at all, and yet, it worked so well that the book has gone into its third edition and has become a recommended read for all architecture students at the Goa College of Architecture. I think part of its success was due to the fact that Gerard never interfered in the process. The only one time that he got involved was when architect Amit Modi (who was working on the line drawings for the book from his office) and I had to make a trip to the Rane House in Sanquelim. I remember the trip rather well less on account of Gerard's driving us there and more on account of his buying us our lunch. We had made a stop at a roadside lunch place somewhere near Tivim. The only item on the menu on offer was omelettes. When our food arrived, Gerard, Amit, and I were in for a surprise. Our omelettes were floating in a muddy brown sea of fish curry accompanied by a small boat of rice. Whatever you chose to eat, lunch in Goa could not be complete without its staple of *xitt kodi,* curry and rice.

Gerard must have been the most non-interfering publisher in the world. The last chapter of the book involved the drawing out of personalities and profiling the homeowners. That was the only chapter that Gerard had taken an interest in. He had left the rest of the writing, research, photo shoots to Annabel and Rukshana and me. Annabel and I wrote one chapter together, the one that had technical details of building. Working with her was a dream. Rukshana and I bonded over being fellow Parsis and accompanying a very fussy Ashok Koshy on the photo shoots in a hired Omni. Not knowing any better, we just assumed that photographers were to be pampered and fussed over because the book would be only as good as the pictures in it.

Rukshana's dad Feroze was our guide and mentor. He would pacify us at the end of an exhausting day's shoot after Ashok had asked for his favourite brand of cigarettes in the middle of salt pans in the blazing Goa heat or had called for a 'pack-up' at three in the afternoon because he had to go get dressed for dinner at ten. Feroze would tell us that all photographers were eccentric and they each had their own quirks, and to get the best results for the book we had to simply grin and bear it. It was good advice for us, of course; we were on a mission but what of the poor driver of the hired car, I wondered. Ashok would often scream at him for not helping him with the lights and the rest of his paraphernalia. 'I need some assistance,' he would bellow at the poor fellow just when he went sliding down on his driver's seat expecting to take a nice long nap.

To his credit, Gerard never once interfered with either our methods or our output. He never once asked for the text while I was writing and only saw the book for the first time when it came back as a first proof copy from the printers in Hyderabad. What's more commendable, he paid me Rs 5,000 every month regularly without my having to ask for it. It was almost like having a job. I would take a motorcycle taxi to his office once the writing was done, and Rukshana and I would sit on one of his office computers and try and put things together.

When Gerard heard about the water problem in the building, he generously allowed me to do my laundry at the office. Nobody in the office thought it odd. Architecture Autonomous was home to a lot of students, interns, and fledgling architects. I would fill a shopping bag with our laundry and sometimes walk all the way to Gerard's office with it, wash during our breaks, and then lug all the clothes back through a lovely little 'short cut' that took me back to Khorlim. Anyone who has carried a shopping bag full of wet laundry to the swishing sound of coconut palms, ripening paddy, and squelching rubber soled slippers will know what I mean.

The book was being written, the photographs were being taken, and the design was taking shape. Our God-fearing landlord at Gangadhar Apartments had had a tiny room built in the flat between the kitchen and the bathroom that was meant to serve as a *puja* room. It had a small window and a marble platform and room for little else. I had made that into my study, my workplace. I would arrange my reference books and my notes and papers against the wall on the little platform and then set my brother typewriter (and later my laptop, a gift from my brother-in-law Rahul in the United States) against my 'bookshelf' and sit on a small plastic bathroom stool. I would work late into the night on some days, and the resonating sound of the typing in that tiny room has still stayed with me.

So has the memory of the night of the cockroaches. Mahrukh and I had a deal. She was terrified of geckos and I had an illogical fear of roaches. It was an understanding between us that if there was a gecko in the house, I would take care of it, and if there was a roach, she would go for the kill and that included cockroach carapaces. The only time this pest extermination failed was when one of us was not in the house or fast asleep. And that is exactly what happened one night. It was warm and I had the little window open. Several cockroaches came flying into my 'study' one after the other. I had a chapter to complete and Mahrukh was fast asleep. I did not have the heart to wake her after a trying day at Wrangler Jeans. I picked up one fat book after another and slammed them on to the insects. I finished the chapter, went to bed, and awoke in the morning only to hear Mahrukh giggling and mock screaming, 'Cockroach!' several times in between picking up cockroach carcasses.

I worked on the book, Mahrukh commuted to Bicholim Industrial Estate, and life at Gangadhar Apartments went on with urban regularity. Our downstairs neighbour's ninety-year old father had a fall and our upstairs neighbour poured a whole bowl of sugar on his bleeding head to stop the bleeding (it worked), another neighbour who worked in the electricity department helped us sort out our overcharged bills (I helped her with her sinuses), and Lynetta Palmeira Sequeira downstairs got pregnant with her second child Larissa.

Unreliable as our little Maruti 800 was, we were the only ones with a car. I had offered to take Lynetta to the hospital for the delivery. Every evening, I would drop in on my hugely pregnant neighbour and ask her if she was all right. Ever cheerful, Lynetta would say she was 'fine'. And then, as expected, there was a knock on our door one night way past midnight. It was Lynetta's husband Keith. I slipped on a pair of shoes, grabbed the car keys, and ran through the door, bundled Lynetta into the car and drove at breakneck speed every few minutes asking her if her water bag had burst. We got to the hospital on time and just before going in, Lynetta asked me a crucial question. 'How did you get dressed so fast?' I just laughed. It was only the next day when we went to see the beautiful little baby that I told her that I had been sleeping in my street clothes all week.

On the other hand, we had a neighbour who happened to be a qualified nurse. Now everyone expected the qualified nurse to come to our assistance once the labour pains began. Lynetta's husband ran to her door and rang the doorbell several times. She did not answer the door. There was no time to waste. We simply bundled Lynetta into the Maruti 800, fired the pistons with a prayer, and headed towards the JMJ Hospital at Porvorim. When the nurse-cum-neighbour came to see the baby, we asked her why she had not answered the doorbell. 'But I had the doorbell switched off.'

'Why?'

'Oh, somebody may ring the bell in the middle of the night, no?'

Of course the whole neighbourhood knew by then that Lynetta had had a daughter. The new baby's grandfather had burst two firecrackers in a row at the summit of the building. It was then that Mahrukh and I knew, for the first time that it was two crackers for a girl and three for a boy. When I discussed this gender discrimination with Fr. Nascimento Mascarenhas at the Archives Department Library the following day, he came up with a tragic-comic story of his own. Fr Nascimento's grandmother who held the reins of the household was expecting her daughter-in-law to deliver a girl after six boys. When Fr. Nascimento was born, she was so disappointed that she would not allow any firecrackers to announce the birth of the boy. Instead, she threw some salt in the wood-fired stove. The salt gave out a half-hearted sizzle, and she turned around to the family and said, 'There! We've told everyone there is another boy.'

Gender discrimination for both Mahrukh and me was something we had had no close links with. Born in female-dominated households, we were brought up to think that men had to be looked after. So as children, we worked hard at our homework, rode bicycles, climbed trees, believed in God, and told ourselves that men were the weaker sex. Living in Goa suited us perfectly. This was one place in India that did not frown on two women living together with no apparent family support or financial dependencies and doing exactly what they wanted to do in life. We could walk around or drive out in our little car at any time of the day or night and feel absolutely safe and unmindful of personal security.

XII

Tea Garden Life in Munnar

'Yes, sir!'

Getting caught in the Bombay riots in 1993 had brought Mahrukh and me closer. We decided to leave Bombay, and our friend Shirin Bharucha helped us get jobs as tea planters (assistant managers) in Tata Tea, Munnar, Kerala. No one had warned us that we were to be India's first women tea planters. We shared a bungalow and worked on separate tea estates under two different managers. Mahrukh would drive to work and then do her rounds of her tea gardens. The fact that Mahrukh was driving out alone ten kilometres each way to her place of work every day of the week was a miracle. Mahrukh had a driving license that she had somehow procured while living with her parents in Nagpur but had never driven a car.

One Friday evening while working in the tea gardens in Munnar, she came back from her estate saying her boss Manjit Singh had asked her to drive to work in the car on Monday. Which assistant manager could argue with his or her manager in the tea world? Every instruction had to be answered with a loud and clear 'Yes, sir!' There was no two ways about it. Besides, no one would believe that a girl who had set out to become one of India's first tea planters, ride a bike over the steep slopes in the tea gardens, hold her own amongst all the other gentlemen planters, and be given honorary membership into the Men's Only Bar at the High Range Club did not know how to drive a car.

So like any other assistant manager, Mahrukh had also said, 'Yes, sir!' when Manjit Singh had asked her to drive to work at the end of the week. Undaunted by this unexpected order, we got to work. I put her in the car and gave her some express driving lessons over the weekend. I took her over the winding roads that took us from estate to town and back several times. By Monday morning, Mahrukh was ready to drive. I must have been a good teacher and she a determined student because not once did anyone on her estate suspect that until that morning their 'lady manager' had never driven a car before in her life.

As for me, I also took one weekend to learn how to get on to my Hero Honda Sleek motorcycle. After walking up to eleven kilometres a day up and down the tea gardens, Mahrukh's manager Manjit Singh made a case for us at their next meeting that we should be given motorcycles for our daily rounds. I had fallen off my cycle as a young girl and had never ridden a two-wheeler after that. I had one weekend to get over that childhood fear. Unlike Manjit, my manager Arun Maharaj never gave orders. He called me in, showed me the new bike and said, 'It's nice of the company to give you a bike, isn't it? Now from Monday you need not walk to the office'. Unlike Mahrukh, I did not click my boot heels and say, 'Yes, sir'. I told him I had never ridden a bike before and that no one had told us when we joined Tata Tea that we would have to learn how to ride a bike. Always polite, Arun Maharaj thought it might be a good idea to try.

We began with skating around the driveway of our tea garden bungalow at Ottoparai, Precious Rock in Sevenmallai, Lord Shiva's mountain doing the figure 8. I would do 8s till I was dizzy and Mahrukh would faithfully run behind me shouting encouragement above the whirring noise of the

Hero Honda engine. Learning how to ride had its funny moments. Not having the physical height to get on to the bike even in my boots, I would have to walk with the bike to a rock or milestone and then climb on to the rock for the extra foothold. By Monday morning, I was able to ride to the office with my heart in my mouth, my planter's hat on my head, and my jaw clamped tight in determination. By the end of the week, I could race up a rocky road up the steep hill slopes, leaving Arun behind at the foot of the hill. Nothing could stop me and that was part of my problem. I had not learnt how to halt properly. Instead of using the brakes on my bike, I would use the trunk of a tree or a rock on the road to teeter dangerously to a halt.

At the end of three months I was the toast of the town for my biking skills. My colleagues (fellow assistant managers) in the twenty-five to twenty-seven age group had finally taken us as 'one of the boys'. They would visit us at our bungalow, corner us at the weekly film screening at the High Range Club, form a protective ring around us in the presence of seniors, and sprinkle us with advice on tea garden social etiquette. At best, the tea estates are far flung from one another; we lived in an insular, outdated, outmoded society isolated from the rest of the world. Living in a 1924 tea garden bungalow and working on a tea estate with all its colonial fall-outs was like living in a time capsule set in the mid-1920s. We were treated like children.

We needed permission from our managers to leave our estates during the day, to leave the tea gardens for weekend trips to Kochi or Coimbatore, and to attend a private dinner party on any other estate after working hours. We even had to get special sanction to be allowed to drive a car when all the other assistant managers were only permitted bikes. Every curry cooked in the house and every butler that rang your dinner gong went through your manager's scrutiny. Mahrukh did not take it all very seriously but I did. So when one of our young colleagues paid us a visit in the late evening, I thought it best 'to confess' to my manager the following morning. Arun was most nonchalant about it. Yes, he knew about it (of course!) and that there was nothing wrong in the visit. Since we possessed neither a television or a video or DVD player nor had a stash of entertaining CDs to play, did he not wonder what our young colleague would find in our Ottoparai bungalow to amuse himself? 'Oh, I know that they only come to you girls for the food,' Arun said. What a relief to be so well understood.

The history of the tea gardens in Munnar is worthy of a book by itself. Mature deciduous forests were cleared to make way for coffee and cinchona at first and then for tea. The first tea garden bungalows were, in fact, small thatched dwellings, too basic to even be called log huts. The first tea planters were Scotsmen who had come out of their own country and pioneered planting in the hills. These hills, once considered forested and 'of no use to man', were once the domain of the tribal chieftain Kanan Devan. The first planters were without doubt men of mettle, self-discipline, and foresight. As the plantations grew, the pioneers needed more men to manage the estates.

In the tea gardens as India's first woman tea planter

That is when trouble began. Rules and regulations had to be made to ensure discipline and obedience. And so, there were rules that prevented you from going to the town and leaving the tea estates over weekends without your manager's permission. There were rules that prevented you from visiting other managers and their families without approval. You were only allowed a holiday (long leave) once in two years. This was reasonable as most 'long leave' was for going home to England in the old days. There were rules that prevented you from sitting down in the presence of your seniors even at social gatherings. Not going to the High Range Club for the weekly entertainment raised eyebrows. Not attending sports meets was frowned upon. As for not being able to play a 'gentleman's sport' like golf, cricket, tennis, squash, bridge, and holding your drink, you would sooner be laughed out of tea.

The curious thing was that long after the last Scotsman had left Munnar, long after tedious sea voyages were not the only way of travelling to England, long after motorcycles had replaced horses as the only way up the hills, nothing had changed. The planting traditions set by the old Scots and the rules and regulations set to discipline young hot-blooded planters were in fact meticulously endorsed by their Indian counterparts. Planters were still addressed respectfully as *dorai,* white masters, and assistant managers were called *chinna dorai*, little white masters.

Although Munnar is located in Kerala, we had to learn to speak Tamil, as most of the labour came from the Tirunelvelli district of Tamil Nadu. When you went for your weekly Tamil language tuition, you were told this story in an effort to improve your diligence: 'Once there was a planter who refused to learn Tamil. One day, he was racing up the hills on horseback and some tea plantation labourers came running to him, holding his stirrups, and telling him in Tamil not to go any further. Not understanding a word of what they were saying, the "white master" kicked a Tamil labourer and went up the hill in full gallop. A huge explosion of dynamite killed him instantaneously. The labourers had been trying to tell him to stop because they had planted dynamite to excavate the hill slopes.'

Needless to say all this happened when 'white masters' still rode horses (we had never seen a horse in Munnar), when there were no 'lady assistant managers', and you were still allowed to kick your Tamil labourers. In any case, we knew that if we did not learn Tamil really quickly, we would be at the mercy of the field officers and assistant field officers to translate for us and that was a disadvantage. True to colonial traditions, field officers were almost always Tamil and assistant field officers Malayalis from Kerala. It was a very cunning device that had been built into the system by the early planters to control the plantations.

Most Scotsmen planters were Freemasons and belonged to the Church of South India. The Tamil-speaking field officers went to the Roman Catholic Church, and the Malayalam-speaking assistant field officers were either 'Marthomites', who went to the Church of St. Thomas or were upper-caste Hindus. The Tamil-speaking labour, all from around Tirunelvelli, were lower-caste Hindus who worshipped at the local Murugan (Kartikeya) temple. Every one of these ethnic groups came with their own built-in prejudices, and like colonists all over the world, the 'gentlemen planters' had turned this to their advantage. Why did the Indian managers and assistant managers who followed the Scots perpetrate this colonial system of control? Why did they, for example, not change the address from *dorai,* white master to the Tamil equivalent of 'manager' or simply, like everywhere in Tamil Nadu, 'sir'?

Hierarchy, of course, was the backbone of the tea estates. The old-style management pyramid had been simplified to the extreme. There were the top managers at the top, then the lower ranking managers at base camp, the new crop of managers making up fresh fodder, and then the field officers, assistant field officers, and at the broadest end of the base, the supervisors and the tea garden labour and bungalow workers. Even estates had their ranks. There were perpetually wet, leech-infested, fog-filled, blight-prone, poor-yielding estates that were damning in their status as punishment postings. Then there were estates where it rained when you wanted it to and shone when you willed it, from where the club was a rum-peg throw away and the trout in the river for the picking. You had to be either really lucky to land such a posting or have come to Munnar under the aegis of a very long benevolent arm. Whatever the estate, you were expected to entertain and be entertained in a rather tea worldly fashion. 'How's the crop?' was the first thing a senior asked you. Your answer depended on whether you perceived the question as benign or malignant. You soon learnt to cram the latest yield figures before going out to dinner. Even at a party, you were expected to stand up with your hands behind your back as if in a witness box and rattle off the latest figures for your fields.

The first piece of advice we received when we arrived was 'Don't think anyone is your friend. Tomorrow he may be your senior, and he may sc*** you!' Well, he really did not have to be your senior to do that, we soon learnt. In the eighteen months that Mahrukh and I were in Munnar, we lost three butlers and a tooth. The butler on the tea estates was actually the cook who also answered the door and helped you out of your mud-caked boots, opened the garage door, and warned you that there were elephants in the vegetable patch. He was indeed a very important man in the bungalow household, usually at the top of the staff pyramid. It was obvious to us that our first butler did not like us. Perhaps he had something against women working as managers; perhaps it was personal. Every night, we would come back tired from walking our eleven kilometres up and down the gardens, and every night he would give us dinner that neither of us recognised as food. Tata Tea had very kindly given us a whole Hitkari dinner set on arrival and the serving dishes had lids. Every night Mahrukh and I would go through this charade of 'You open the lid and I will tell you what's under'. 'No, you open the lid'.

I was lucky with my manager Arun Maharaj and his wife Viji. Not heeding advice, we trusted them, and our friendship has outlived our stint at Munnar. It was the same with Mahrukh's manager Manjit Singh and his wife Devika as well. I finally got so frustrated with the butler's antics that I complained to Arun. Arun immediately arranged for the butler to be transferred, and we began a search for a new one. The second butler turned out to be a spy. He would sneak around the house, reporting every falling leaf, every mouse that ran down the fireplace chimneys, and every log of wood that went crackling in the living room fireplace. Wood was rationed to us in the tea garden bungalows and its usage monitored and reported. Since the old stove in the bungalow kitchen used firewood and the monsoons and winters in Munnar were unbearably cold without a fire, unexpected guests would sometimes see us wrapped up in our blankets in the formal living room, eating *thaeir soup,* spiced hot yoghurt in a bowl.

Not that we had many unexpected guests. While in Munnar, you almost always had to report a visit and you most certainly had to take your manager's permission if you had house guests. Permission once given you had to promise to turn your guests out on the third day even if they were family. Munnar was the most favoured holiday destination for all our Bombay friends and we had a flurry of friends and acquaintances, even fellow journalists and people who had simply heard of us, and were surprised to hear that we had stolen away from Bombay and had headed for the hills. Curious, suspicious, or envious of our motives in leaving the city (I remember my bank manager saying, 'No one ever leaves Bombay. Please tell me the *real* reason for why you are closing this bank account.') Bombay simply followed us all the way to Munnar.

Whether our new butler got tired of our steady stream of guests or fed up of our pleas to cook without red hot spices, I shall never know, but he did have me head to the dentist's chair. The cooked rice had been enriched with some real heavy metal, and one of the stones had broken a tooth. I can still remember the agony of dental surgery, and I can tell you that it was nothing compared to the daily drill of sampling his cooking. I found myself scouring recipe books over weekends and making strawberry flans and apple strudels, baking pizzas, bread and sponge cakes from scratch, and for all this, I must declare my eternal gratitude to my cooking mentor Devika, Manjit Singh's ever-affectionate and caring wife. Finally, the gardener came to our rescue much in defiance of 'company' rules and helped us with his now famous *parottas.* My brother and his boys still remember Karpaswamy's Ceylonese *parotta.* They say that they have never eaten such *parotta* since.

Life in the bungalows was not all struggling to get the perfect meal. Besides being a near-perfect cook, Karpaswamy was an expert dancer. For what else could one call his 'Sunday Twist'? Every weekend, Karpaswamy would prepare two thick pads from sacking cloths, sew them with some strong twine, and then dig his feet into these pads to polish the floors. Both Mahrukh and I were convinced that our Karpaswamy had a drummer inside his head because the rhythm, with which he twisted and turned, slid on the straight paths, and pirouetted round the corners, was palpable. When he did that, I was reminded of the houseboy at my friends Sherna and Keki Wadia's home in Dar es Salaam, Tanzania. The Wadias also had parquet floors in their home that needed polishing. Keki must have indeed had a lot of spare innerwear because their African houseboy would pile up what looked like five pairs of old innerwear under his feet and polish the floors dancing to the drummer in *his* head.

While Mahrukh's field officer had asked her to cram the botanical names of all the weeds in the fields, a totally useless exercise, my field officer filled me in with love stories from the labour lines. With erratic butlers sprinkling our food with stones and a varied range of experiences with our field officers the new addition to our Munnar tea garden bungalow came in like a breath of fresh air. Geeta Mary was as beautiful and gentle as her name suggested. Our managers decided that since we were 'lady assistants', we were entitled to an ayah to look after us and save ours from becoming an all-male household. Geeta Mary took over our lives. She ran halfway across the garden when we arrived for lunch just so she could be the first to get our boots off. She picked leeches off our ankles without missing a count (some days twenty-four); she pressed our clothes for parties, oiled our hair over weekends, helped with the herb garden, and kept her eyes and ears open for any rumblings in the ranks. She knew the sound of every bike in the estates and could tell who was riding up to the bungalow long before it arrived. She watched my bike riding like a football coach watching over a toddler in a park, and when I went straight into a tree trunk, she scolded me in Tamil, saying, 'Amma, you were riding so nicely until this moment.'

Our home sparkled with her touch and now with freshly polished floors, nicely washed curtains, and fuchsias clambering up the stone columns in the porch, we were ready for our annual inspection. Another fallout of the colonial era, all tea garden bungalows went through an annual inspection from one of the senior managers at the regional office when, accompanied by your own manager, the senior would inspect your garden (the sweet peas were nodding to attention), look up and down the trees (the cherry blossoms were in bloom and showering petals on the dignitaries) stand under the passion fruit bowers (they were in bloom too with their beautiful purple flowers in state), and then stride into the bungalow for a closer look at every room, nook, and cranny in the house.

All the furniture was in place, all the beds covered to points of decency, bathrooms smelled like wild roses, the old wood-fired stove gleamed in its station, the chimneys had been swept clean, and none of the grime, dust, or mice that we had seen in our dark bad butler days was visible. I think we passed the test with flying colours except for a few remarks about the garden not being filled with flowers. 'I thought you said she ran a plant nursery in Bombay,' I remember Vijay Kumar saying on the aside. Perhaps he had no idea that my plant nursery in Bombay sold only Bombay balcony-worthy ornamentals and that most of the city customers at the nursery asked for 'plants that needed no sunlight'. 'Perennials and seasonals' therefore were magical words for us that only jumped out of books written by the English.

There were other inspections too, of a different kind. They say that elephants never forget, and I believe it to be true. There was an old elephant track going past our bungalow and through what was now the butler's house. Our constant battle to discipline our butlers and coerce them into moving into the butler's quarters had been in vain. They all had insisted on sleeping in the kitchen, and one night, well past the midnight hour, we finally knew the reason for this 'insubordination'. Geeta Mary crept into our bedroom and woke us up with the one and only important word in the tea gardens. '*Yanai*'. Elephant. Mahrukh and I swept out into the side verandah, expecting to see the elephants claim their own old pathway and demolish the butler's quarters as they went about staking their claim.

There must have been about ten female elephants on our pathway. The moon was full, and they had just walked through some water in the rivulet below before climbing up the hill. 'See, now you know,' says the butler with a smug expression on his face. Yes, now we knew; we acknowledged expecting the rampage to begin. Unafraid of the gentle-looking animals, we decided to get a little closer, forgetting years of training to stay camouflaged and under cover. We forgot that Mahrukh was in an electric pink nightdress and matching gown. In the moonlight, her bright fair face (she is not called Mahrukh or moon face for nothing) and the pink nightgown must have been too much for the elephants to take. They did a right about turn, having forgotten that they had come on a demolition mission. Perhaps electric pink nightgowns were the solution to the 'elephant problem' in the tea gardens.

Matters in the tea gardens were not always resolved so peaceably. The most dangerous reputation belonged to the dholes or wild dogs. They hunted in packs and were known, just like the Indian bison, to attack without provocation. Dholes, we were told, would slowly form an unseen circle around you, and then with one squeaky signal from their pack leader they would attack. It was a beautiful Sunday morning and I had decided to walk into the tea gardens, looking for straying calves. Calves in the fields meant dung pats, which, in turn, meant more weeds in the tea. Sunday mornings were also filled with encounters with wandering gangs of labour leaders. The wandering gangs would be on the lookout for masses of weeds in the tea. They would then point those out to you and recommend an eradication programme that they would then get paid for. That is when I saw what looked like a handsome dog with his golden fur shining like a Hollywood star's on Sunset Boulevard.

Luckily for me, a gang of labour leaders were there at the same time, in the same field. They were not supposed to be there, of course, but this was not the time to go by the book. I called out to one of them by name (not strictly kosher. We were only to address our labour through their supervisors and never by their first names, but I had broken that rule by several degrees already) and shouted, *'Naayee'*. Dog. Quick to action, the men spread out in circular motion, sticks appearing out of nowhere, and began shouting and screaming. The handsome animals simply looked at them in disdain and walked off like children interrupted by adults in a game. I was almost saddened to see them go. If dholes could laugh, they were laughing all the way into the forest corridor that day. I don't think the labour leaders had the least impact on them.

The corridor was what we called the forest that had been left undisturbed on the ridge of every hill that Tata Tea owned or managed. The history of the tea gardens is the history of the colonisation of the country. Pioneering Scotsmen had arrived to tame the wild land and 'civilise' the 'natives'. They had acquired forested lands under long-term leases from the local tribal leaders and cleared the forests and planted cinchona trees to yield quinine that cured malaria, then tried out coffee, and finally planted tea. Private tea planters, impoverished and living on the brink of survival for the most part of their enterprise, were then 'bought over' by Finlays, a British company that became Tata-Finlay and finally Tata Tea Ltd. When I was at Munnar, Tata Tea owned a conglomerate of 11,000 square kilometres of tea.

Whether out of a real sense of consideration for wild animals or simply to keep them out of the tea, the corridor was kept untouched. We would often go there to watch the Malabar Giant Squirrel leap up and down the trees. We would also go up to look at the tea trees that had been allowed to grow to unimaginable heights of fifteen metres and beyond. Tea, we realised, could grow to immense heights if left alone. It is only when it is cultivated as a cash crop that it is kept stunted to 'bush' height and pruned by hand plucking or shearing. In fact, one of the main aims of tea garden managements is to maintain a *muttom,* table that allows for maximum spread and even growth thus optimising bush yield.

The Corridor had many thrills to offer. The one that was the most thrilling was when wire tailed swallows dipped and turned in the air, and you could hear the swish of their wings against your ear. I can still hear a *zing* when I think about it. There were other sounds too. There was the rattle of a helicopter that flew over the corridor once in a while on lazy Sunday afternoons. The helicopter would drop what looked like a hammock and then bales of what looked like grass would be loaded on to the hammock. What those bales of grass were was anybody's guess but we had learnt very quickly that there were times when you learnt nothing new by asking the wrong questions. Munnar still has the best 'grass' in India.

On the other hand, there were times when you did ask the right question. On one of my walks up the hills, I had seen a water tank fairly overgrown with weeds and other vegetation, wildflowers growing on its sides, and creepers cascading down its cracking algae-filled concrete. All the water tanks in the tea gardens were designed to collect water from passing streams and the water directed into the bungalows, quarters, and labour lines through galvanised pipes. The higher the location of the water tanks, the more uncontaminated it was assumed to be. If any wild animals drank from the tank, we just assumed they were clean. I used to inspect all the tanks regularly, swelling with pride that I was ensuring good clean water for 'my people' on the estate. I had quite clearly missed this one on my regular inspections. I called Biju, the assistant field officer to attention the following morning and marched him up to the errant tank. 'Where is this water being supplied?' I asked him in my most officious tone. 'To your bungalow, madam,' he said clicking his heels *his* most officious.

The love-hate relationship one shared with the field officers and assistant field officers in the tea gardens was different from any other anywhere else. Redefined in the tea gardens, it meant that if the field officer loved you, his assistant hated you, and if the assistant loved you, his senior hated you. It was inevitable. You often felt like you were caught in a bind with them. On the one hand, they were the only buffers you had between the tea garden labour and yourselves. When you first arrived and could not speak any Tamil, calculate daily wages on the tips of your fingers, or could not tell the bewitched from the easily possessed, your only friend, philosopher or guide was your field officer. If you insisted on punctuality, he was the one who reminded you that your workers landed up in the fields before dawn on days when the crop was plenty. If you wanted to wander into a secret garden meeting of female workers, he was the one who warned you that there would be women there playing at being possessed by evil spirits.

It was your field officer who introduced you to the curious tea garden practice of workers showering you with fresh lemons as tokens of appreciation or welcome. He was also the one who shared his favourite lime pickle recipes with you at the end of the explanation. He was also the one who titillated you with stories of how, in the days of yore, a planter would casually leave his hat on a particular row of tea bushes and expect the tea garden worker to follow him into his bedroom. He was the one who frightened you with stories of how, if you annoyed your workers, they would surround you and then flick hundreds of leeches at you. He was the one who advised you against planting maize, sugarcane, and bamboo in the bungalow garden so as to not attract elephants. He was the one who divided all the managers into three main categories (office managers, garden managers, and factory managers), depending on what each manager liked to do best. He would mournfully say, 'We field officers are like the proverbial curry leaf. You cannot cook without the curry leaf, and yet just when you are about to put the food in your mouth, you take the leaf out and throw it. That is who we are. The curry leaves that you throw out just before you enjoy your meal . . .' I used to think that was an original from my field officer until I shared it with Manjit and Devika and Manjit said to me, 'Every Field Officer in Munnar says this to get your unconditional sympathy.'

Every manager had his own plantation story to add spice to our lives. Here are some of my favourites: Manjit married Devika in Delhi and brought her on a train to Kochi to begin her life as a tea garden bride. As she was getting off the train, her entire trousseau crammed into several large suitcases and boxes, she was met with by an assemblage of tea garden workers, all men in crisp starched white shirts and *dhotis*, all carrying a black umbrella each. Impressed by the turnout, she expected them to pay obeisance and begin carrying out her assortment of packages. Instead, every one of the workers who had come to see their new *amma*, mistress, put out a hand and began offering her anything from four to ten lemons. 'Manjit', she screamed, 'what is wrong with your fellows? Here I need help with my bags and instead of helping me, all they are doing is giving me these *nimboos*?'

The other one of my favourite stories is the one where a manager walked past the wildlife corridor to get to a tea garden and meet with his field officer. When he met his field officer, he was told that he had just walked past a 'lone tusker'. Now in tea garden parlance, this was a dangerous proposition indeed. A 'lone tusker' is a single young male elephant in his prime, with fully developed tusks, sometimes in *musth*, often bad-tempered and certainly not worth taking any chances with. When the manager asked the field officer why he had not been warned about the 'lone tusker', the field officer smartly answered, 'Not a lone tusker, *saar*, he had two tusks!'

Then there is the story of an assistant manager returning from a late-night party up in Kundalai about two hours away from the lower Munnar tea fields. The story is that he sees this lone tusker standing in the middle of the road right in front of their car, facing them, his eyes burning in their headlights. Imagining that they were seeing things in the dark, they just stopped and decided to wait it out. The lone tusker charged. It was probably a mock charge, but it scared the living daylights out of the manager and his companion. They whipped their doors open and went scrambling into the storm ditch on the side of the road. When they did not hear anything further, one of them braved a look. What he saw astonished him beyond belief. The young male elephant had walked up to the car (a small red Maruti 800) turned around and had seated himself on the bonnet. 'We did not know if we should be amused or amazed,' said he as he recounted the story. 'He just sat there, nonchalant, on the bonnet for close to two hours, and we half expected him to sit there and have a smoke!' Satisfied with his night's work, the young fellow then simply walked away from the scene, leaving the assistant manager and his companion with a sense of shock, relief, and a huge repair bill.

Manjit was offered a post-retirement post in coffee after nearly thirty-seven years in tea. 'As assistants, we used to play such terrible tricks,' he recalls with a mischievous grin. 'If our senior wanted to visit a particular tea field and it happened to be in very poor shape, all we did was get some old elephant dung, heap it on the field road and pour some hot water on it. We would then point to the steaming dung and pretend that an elephant (or a herd of elephants if the field was really bad) had just walked into the field, and it was therefore dangerous to be there. The advantage of having been so devious is that now if someone tries to play the same trick on me, I can catch them out at once!' he laughs.

Another Manjit favourite story is the one of the factory manager who was asked to entertain some government officials at the tea factory. In the middle of the night, Manjit was pulled out of bed with a jangling phone call from the factory manager. He was in a state of distress. 'Sir!' he screamed in Tinglish (Tamil English) into the phone, 'These officials are not at all reasonable, sir. They are wanting some wine and some womens (sic) and some *biryani* also! At this time of the night, how can I arrange for the *biryani*, sir?'

As he worked up the ladder, Manjit sometimes had to entertain senior managers and directors from other Tata companies. He says he had taken a senior director from one of the Tata companies on a picnic to the exquisite Devikulam Lake in the picturesque Idukki district of Kerala. This natural lake had been expanded by Sir John Muir in 1895 as a recreational area for the tea planters to go fishing and hunting. The hosts had laid on the works for this very important guest. There were several assistants in attendance, a sumptuous picnic lunch, and there was also the director's special young friend. Now Manjit was trying to explain to his guests that the lake held a special significance to the local Tamil population. It was believed to be the Lake where Sita *mai*, Lord Rama's chaste wife, had bathed and planted some rice (while being abducted by King Ravana) en route to Sri Lanka. The surrounds also yielded wild mushrooms locally called *kozhukatta*. In more recent history, and diverse from the *Ramayana* legend, the dense forests around Devikulam also had historic significance.

The ruins of the Sir Arthur Wellesley Fort at Devikulam were hardly visible from where the picnic party was, but nevertheless, Manjit decided to entertain his guests by giving them a dose of local history. Colonel Wellesley (later the Duke of Wellington) had set up camp here where there was once a pond and cattle track. Records say that the Nilgiri tahr (ibex) was so tame in those days that the soldiers stuck bayonets into these unfortunate animals to amuse themselves. Locals recall the spot and remember it as the site where Wellesley had set up an ambush and waited in vain for the wily Tipu Sultan. Pleased with his own knowledge of local history, Manjit expected an intelligent response from his guests. Instead, the sweet young thing accompanying the director piped up and said, 'Oh, so Tipu made off with Sita, is it?' For all his efforts, Manjit was rewarded with a terse command the following day. 'Kindly do not accompany the guests in the future as they need time to themselves on holiday.'

Like the managers of Munnar, visitors to the tea gardens too had their own stories to tell. My friend Deepa Bajekal Joshi paid a visit to Munnar with her late mother and stayed with one of the managers in a spectacularly beautiful tea estate. While they were there, Deepa says there was much social flurry over this highly reputed photographer who was also touring those parts, and her hostess decided to invite the photographer over for tea. Out came the lace doilies, the damask tablecloths, the runners on the dressing tables, the guest towels with their delicately embroidered flowers done by the nuns in the Munnar Convent, the best china and silver. There were cakes iced by the hostess herself, fresh strawberries in a freshly baked flan, and biscuits turned out on the British-made wood-fired stove. Everything was set to perfection, down to the last zinnia in the crystal vase when the esteemed guest walked in dressed in his field clothes and smelling like one of God's own creatures. At the end of the tea, Deepa's shattered hostess was left wondering aloud if the sofa covers needed changing and if the spoons had to be sterilised.

Being a tea garden wife is not the easiest of jobs. First of all, you have to adhere to an undefined pecking order in tandem with your husband's hierarchy status, and just like him, you too cannot cement any real friendships. Alienated from your husband's tea garden life, you live the day separated from him for the most part, growing flowers in the bungalow garden and looking forward to the next annual flower show. You have to learn how to manage a home on a budget, entertain regularly and with precision while you nervously walk on social eggshells, raise the kids in an isolated, insular society, make your mark on Munnar's High Range Club, and, worse, behave like you were surrogate employees of a company that does not permit you to work outside your home even if you are a trained professional.

When we arrived in Munnar as India's first women tea planters, Mahrukh and I were met with a variety of reactions that ranged from surprise to sarcasm. The initial curiosity then gave way to open resentment and some of the younger wives, clearly fed up of being 'thanked for the flowers' at the end of every social function, began to make a demand for their own space. 'If these two women can come out here and work as tea planters, then why should we not be given an opportunity to work as well?' was the general drift that finally reached the ears of Ratna Krishnakumar, at Tata Tea top brass level. Luckily for everyone concerned, Ratna did not live in an ivory tower. She visited us regularly in Munnar, and all she did when she was there was keep her eyes and ears open. I don't think I had ever met a better listener than Ratna. It was from her that I learnt that listening is both an art and a skill.

Ratna not just kept her eyes and ears open; she actually went out of her way to meet the tea garden wives. She soon realized that they would have a rebellion on their hands if they did not do something about the rumblings. Ratna took the bull by the horns, felt the pulse of the people, and gripped the tightrope with her toes. Munnar had traditions that were over 150 years old that had to be held sacrosanct and yet one had to move with the times. These were Munnar residents, its backbone who, even unknown to themselves, were holding these traditional systems together. Some of these traditions were decades behind the times, but all the managers and their wives individually and collectively made an effort to hold these together. There was safety and security in continuum. After prolonged and pleasant interactions, Ratna steered all available talent into a highly professional food processing unit (marketed all over India as High Range products), a natural dye workshop (with its garments being retailed at the Kurunji shop in Munnar) and a separate school for the tea garden children with special needs. She nurtured those who were interested and gave them an opportunity to hone their skills with training and interactive workshops.

In a year's time since she first began working with the Munnar ladies, Ratna had wiped the furrows of suspicion and dissent and had infused a new sense of ownership and belonging into the lives of the wives of Munnar. If governments were to adapt the same method, there would be no need for voluntary organisations.

XIII

Goa Heritage Action Group

'What is heritage?'

In Goa, however, things were quite different. When we arrived in Goa in the middle of the 1995 monsoon, voluntary work could not have been further away from our minds. Survival was the preoccupation, and I knew that working for an NGO meant a further drain on personal resources. Besides, everything looked so beautiful, so perfect. We did not think anything could be wrong in this paradise. Five years later and once Mahrukh had left Goa for Nagpur, my lotus-eating days came to a close. Gerard had asked me to work on *Houses of Goa*, and I began to see chinks in front facades of the houses. Everyone was putting on an act. There were so many things that were awry; it was time to do something.

I started the Goa Heritage Action Group in Goa in October 2000 from a one-bedroom 500 square feet apartment in Porvorim, typing out letters of appeal and protest on my own manual typewriter. I lived on a single *poi,* the traditional Goan whole wheat bread, for breakfast and boiled cabbage for lunch. I had no idea then how long I'd be staying in Goa, how long the group would last, or how long I would last in a group in Goa. Typically, I had no plans, not for myself and not for the group. Of only one thing I was certain and it was that I would quit this group after two years and hand over the reins to a local ethnic Goan. I had left Mumbai after nine and a half years of being in the forefront of the heritage movement in the city, and I had no intention of repeating that history here or replicating that experience.

The Mumbai years had only ended in heartache and pain. From what friends holidaying in Goa from Mumbai were saying, the Indian Heritage Society of which I had been a part was rife with internecine battles, vicious competitiveness, and fickle friendships after our Chairman and mentor Sohrabji had passed on. *If every group that you are part of has to end this way, then what point was there in setting something up in a new place*, I wondered. I decided to set up the Goa group only because I thought that someone from the newly formed group would hedge me out someday soon and I would then be free to go my own way.

How did we build this image of the Goa Heritage Action Group in a state that is really only as big or as small as two districts in, say, Maharashtra? I think the greatest advantage I had was that I could start on a virgin slate. 'What is heritage?' asked environmental Patricia Pinto who I had met in Mapusa in environmentalist Claude Alvares's office in Mapusa. My work in Mumbai and elsewhere in Maharashtra had followed me here, and Claude had made the fatal error of introducing me as a 'heritage activist from Bombay'. How could a Goan environmentalist, meeting over a campaign to stop the quarrying of rock and earth and of the destruction of mangroves, not know that heritage preservation is very much part of the environmental movement? That when you demolish an existing structure, you are actually destroying building material and intellectual property of the builders and then making matters worse by going out into the countryside and quarrying more rocks and earth to replace what you have just destroyed?

Besides, we had met in Mapusa, a border town that resembled nothing close to the Goa of the tourist brochures that the Government of Goa so loves its tourists to see. Blind walls stare you in the face when you enter the town. The town had no character. In a nutshell, there was nothing Goan about Mapusa except perhaps the weekly Friday market. Shops and indiscriminate concrete blocks had been allowed to come up in the town, and the planning norms that one would normally expect to be in place were conspicuously absent. Mapusa, to me, was like a town under siege and rapid urbanisation was the enemy within. In Mapusa, Goa had lost its frontiers. There was, however, a note of optimism. In between concrete high rises, that stood right in front of heritage buildings like giant cement blinds, there were some houses and shops that chronicled its history. Somebody should do something to save these vestiges of Goan history, I said to myself. Only, I did not know that that somebody would have to be me.

When I thought of starting the group, I felt that I had actually stepped into a time machine. The arguments that we had been up against in Mumbai in 1982-3 were the same. I would have to reinvent the wheel. Considering that I had put in over eleven years with Shyam Chainani, the 'best in the business' of preservation, I thought that I simply had to apply the same template and it would work. I was wrong. Every time I applied a facet of the old template, mimicked the same methods, or applied the same arguments that I had learnt at Shyam's feet in Mumbai, I met with roadblocks that I had never encountered before. Government responses defied logic and so-called like-minded people were giving me 'the look'.

The one and only environmental group that I had met so far said that they had their hands full. I don't think they had made the connection between heritage and the work they were doing in environmental protection. So when Raya Shankhwalker introduced me to his colleague Poonam Verma Mascarenhas, a north Indian married to a Goan former Indian Air Force officer, I was absolutely thrilled. Raya, Poonam, and I met at Poonam's Caranzalem flat and planned out a simple strategy. We would approach concerned government officials asking for meetings and explain why we felt that Goa needed heritage regulations. I was accustomed to approaching governments through its bureaucracy. While working with

Shyam Chainani in the Bombay Environmental Action Group in Mumbai that is how we had done it. And that is how I thought it would work here too. To us in Mumbai, we breathed heritage protection.

All the bureaucrats came from the same Indian Administrative Services. Every one of them had the power to convince their ministries. Wrong. All the letters we wrote were simply assigned to the state dustbin. The secretaries and collectors that we met were, as we discovered over time, waiting either for plum postings in Delhi or were biding their time on holiday before they retired. A young collector was frank enough to look out of the window one morning, as we were speaking to him, saying, 'I am here only for the view.' This was frustrating business indeed. Who then was running the state? As it turned out, it is the ministers and the chief ministers. They have quite simply carved up the state like a fiefdom with territories marked out and shared amongst them.

It soon became obvious that public action meant something quite different in Goa. One day Patricia Pinto called to say they were organising a protest to stop the local government from cutting down some mature rain trees in Campal. Would I come? The whole protest meeting was like a family picnic. It was a Sunday afternoon, and Patricia and members of her family were there. Their friends dropped by with snacks, water bottles, and music. Students followed with drumbeats; somebody brought a poem they had written on the trees. There were balloon sellers to amuse the children, an ice-cream man to help you cool off, and lots of singing, dancing, and clapping. It was miles away from any protest meeting I had ever been to. And it worked. The trees got saved (for a while at least), and Patricia became a hero. When Jaimini Mehta, principal of the Goa College of Architecture, also an outsider like me, walked up to me and said, 'I was preparing myself for some police brutality. Is this a protest meeting?' All we could do was laugh. Nevertheless neither Jaimini nor I saw ourselves organising 'picnic protests' like these. So I just carried on with the letter writing and the liaisons with heritage-friendly bureaucrats, however short-lived their Goa stints were and however much they were enjoying the view.

While these futile attempts were being made on the one hand, I also had to keep one eye on my household budget. Mahrukh and I had rented out a one-room farmhouse at Mr Farmer's on the National Highway that ran between Mapusa and Guirim in North Goa. The book on *Houses of Goa* was over and done with and the Rs 160-Rs 250 that the regular stories to the *Navhind Times* and the *Gomantak Times* did not take us very far. The pressure to find some sort of assignment that would keep us going was immense.

My most recent work was the listing of heritage bungalows and historic artefacts in the tea gardens with Tata Tea. I had resigned after my motorcycle accident, but Mahrukh still had to fulfil a three-month notice period before she would be allowed to leave. Not wanting to seem like a burden on the company that had given us such a unique opportunity, I offered to do the only thing I knew I was good at.

Tata Tea had close to 155 heritage bungalows and some very fine historic artefacts that dated to the First World War. As the assistant manager at Sevenmallay Tea Estate I would visit these bungalows and write an article for the Tata Tea in-house magazine *Saithigal*. I asked the company directors if I could do a more complete job by surveying the bungalows I had not yet covered in the magazine. Tata Tea gave me a car, a driver, and a photographer, and I had set about doing a comprehensive listing of the tea garden bungalows of Munnar, Kerala. The results were a very nice documentation of all the properties in Tata Tea.

Remembering that, my pauper status in Goa gave me an idea. What if I did the listing of heritage properties for the rest of Kerala? That would help me survive. As they say, luck favours the foolish. Just then, Shyam happened come to Goa for a conference. It was to be the first and last attempt by the Town & Country Planning Department, Goa at a discussion on regulations for Goa's heritage. I was sent an invitation. In the lobby of the Cidade Goa hotel, Shyam asked me if I could carry this Tata Tea assignment forward and take it to Kochi and the Greater Kochi Region (six districts around Kochi) as the Ministry of Environment and Forests, Government of India, was doing a carrying capacity study of the region. Dr S. C. Maudgal, senior scientific officer in the ministry, was very keen that heritage properties be included in the study. I jumped at it and went down by train to Kochi, was hosted by the Tourism Department, and did the listing. I received a modest sum of money. We now had enough to live on.

Tragedy strikes when one is least expecting it. Just when I thought that all was going well with the preparation for the Kerala book, Dr Maudgal passed away, and there was no one in the department who knew of me. Spending my meagre savings on phone calls to Delhi proved futile. There had simply been no paperwork on the subject. In other words, neither I nor my assignment existed in the ministry. I had foolishly relied on a personal assurance from a friend in the ministry, a mistake that I was to make repeatedly. My photographer friend Farah Vakil accompanied me to Kochi on my last trip to Kerala to take the pictures. With a personal reference from Cyrus Guzder in Mumbai, I showed the results to Amitav Ghose, then secretary of Tourism (who sat at a desk smaller than his own personal assistant's) and convinced him to publish it in a book. He took all of five minutes for him to tell me that the department did not publish anything but he could give me the publishing job if I had a publishing house.

I went out of his room and came back in ten minutes. We now had a publishing house. That is exactly how The Heritage Network, a name suggested by Farah, was born. What photographs that needed retaking, Poonam and her husband Walter finished for us in their little blue Maruti 800 with some help from friends in Tata Tea. The Heritage Guide to Kerala, a small pocket-sized book was printed in Mumbai on a shoestring budget. On the personal front, Mahrukh left Goa and moved back with her family in Nagpur. I started making more frequent trips to Mumbai to see my parents. Amitav Ghose had also moved on, to Delhi, but Kerala being Kerala, the director of Tourism saw to it that both Farah and I were invited to the launch of the book and treated to an overnight stay in a rice boat on the Kerala backwaters. We did not let it bother us that *A Heritage Guide to Kerala* was launched along with the inauguration of a public toilet.

Pleased as punch at the success of the Kerala guide, I expected Goa to take a little notice. On the contrary, the people who knew about my work on the Kerala guide became even more suspicious of my intentions. In fact, as to be expected from this xenophobic little state, they took umbrage when I would say, 'Goa is special, but I work for the preservation of heritage where ever I live.' I stopped giving copies of the little guide book around as samples. Instead, I began really looking around for ideas of how to get more people in Goa to believe in the value of their own heritage. I also began to put my ego on the back burner and started taking money from my parents. I had a backlog of apologies to make and a neat little pile up of hitherto untouched inheritance. My adventures had somehow drawn me closer to my parents, and I was getting more drawn to my own personal history and heritage.

XIV

Life at Tehmi Terrace

'Perhaps I was groomed to be single by both parents.'

Dad had retired from service in Baroda long before I came back from Tanzania. Grandma Tehmina had been laid to rest, and my parents with my brother had moved to Tehmi Terrace, the Bandra house. As a child, I had always dreamed of living in this house, and for some reason in my childhood fantasy, the house was always filled with women. Is it possible for a house to have feelings? Not a girl anymore myself and with friends of both genders in and out of the house, I still feel that Tehmi Terrace is happiest when filled with the sounds of free-spirited women.

Two months after Mum passed away, I was asked to answer a few questions on the house in Bandra by a writer who was researching heritage houses in Mumbai. As I began to answer her questions on the house, I opened up to Chandrima Pal and began to answer questions that she had not even asked. I began to tell her how close I had been to my parents, how Mum had supported me right through my career as an environmentalist and heritage conservationist, a career that had been a drain on her time and money. I began to tell her how my work and my acts of gratitude towards my generous parents had outlived every personal relationship or friendship I had ever had. The friendships had survived, yes, but only the ones that my mother had approved of. The relationships had all died a premature death simply because both my parents had always managed to find something 'ugly', something 'missing' in anybody I had brought home to dinner. I was allowed lots of friends provided my mother also liked them. She made certain that no single friend occupied a central place on my social landscape.

'Perhaps I was groomed to be single by both parents,' I said to my interviewer and now my confidant. 'Perhaps I was raised by them as insurance against their old age.' I had only voiced what had long been embedded in my subconscious, but I think I jolted both interviewer and myself. Before Chandrima recovered from the shock of that confession, I quickly jumped to my parents' rescue and justified their manipulation. I was happy they had done that, I smiled lopsidedly, and that had allowed me to pursue my own passions without the distractions of marriage, children, and the pursuit of money. It had worked out perfectly. While they were in their middle age and still active, they were able to support me in my pursuits of happiness. When they became older, troubled with illness, I had reached a point when I was ready to retract from my voluntary work. Their illness became an excuse to get out of Goa. I was disillusioned. Both my parents were delighted that I could come back to Mumbai to see them more often, and if Dad had not been afflicted by the dreadful Alzheimer's disease, I am certain he would have said, 'I told you so.'

The more Dad forgot, the more Mum remembered. She began to tell me the story of how she met Dad, how she fell in love with him after the rescue of the calf from the village well, and how her parents were 'dead against' her marrying an outsider, a 'non'. This period of defiance and the hardship that followed soon took its toll. Mum became physically ill and had to be admitted into the Mission Hospital at Wai where she lay for several months. Her parents soon relented and brought her to the Bandra house and then to the house in Siganpore from where she was taken to the Parsi Sanatorium at Dumas to recuperate. It was at Dumas that she met my father once again. They spent many afternoons together walking up and down the beach at Dumas, considered a resort in those days.

One thing led to another, and Mum and Dad made their intentions to marry known. Both her parents opposed the match vehemently. She mortgaged Abbas Villa to Dad's uncle and paid for his PhD at Texas much before they were married. The rent from the small house in Dhobi Gully and the sporadic rent from vacationers at Abbas Villa was her only source of private income. While Dad was busy getting a research degree in the United States, Mum was forced into a marriage she did not want and was imprisoned in the two rooms upstairs by her mother when she threatened to run away to Abbas Villa, the house in Panchgani that had always been her best friend. It was in those trying times that Tehmi Terrace became her only solace. She was permitted to walk on the mosaic floors of the terrace, but she was to stay confined to the two rooms upstairs.

Grandma Tehmina occupied all of the first floor, guarding herself against intruders with a heavy collapsible gate. She would never cook at home, going out once a week to the Ratan Tata Institute to collect her food supplies. She had the old Chevrolet parked in the garage but never went out in it. She had a driver, Shankar, who had nowhere else to be and drank French polish out of a tin. There were copious supplies of the polish in the storerooms. Anisa from the neighbourhood came over once in a while to sweep the floors. Grandma trusted no one and entertained nobody. When Grandfather had to go into town and look up the timetable that would tell him when his ship was to sail for Aden, he took a bus. Grandma's favourite red Chevrolet was considered too fragile to be taken into town.

'*Muwa Mumbai ney aag lage,*' Grandma would curse. May the cursed Mumbai burn down in a fire. She hated the city and would have moved to Panchgani but did not do that because her daughter now owned the house. My guess is that she must have feared that if the mortgage was not paid, even Mum would lose the house to complete strangers and more so to non-Parsis or *parjaats*. Dad did come back from Texas. He got himself a government job (at that time the only job that gave you security and that is why often referred to as 'job security') and came barging into Tehmi Terrace, got Mum's release from her prison upstairs, and had the marriage to the Parsi husband annulled. Once free, she married her 'American returned' hero in 1953 and began a new chapter in life. Meanwhile, Grandfather, troubled by the harsh South Yemen heat, returned to India with debilitating skin disorders. Never having had a formal education, hospitals and English-speaking doctors intimidated him. He surrendered to a ghastly experiment in a small clinic in Poona where they injected him with large doses of pure iodine. The pain of that administration was too much for him to bear and he took to his bed after that.

In an attempt to make peace and reconciliation with his only child, Grandfather sent for Mum and was delighted when he saw she was expecting a baby. After that Mum visited him every day and tried to make his life as comfortable as was possible within her limited means. She took him to an *ayurvedic* doctor and a *unani* practitioner for the skin ailments. There was some relief for the skin sores, but the *unani* doctor warned his patient that he had a weak heart and that he should see a heart specialist. Grandfather ignored the warning. He continued to tuck into his breakfasts of *bheja per eida,* fried eggs over sheep brains, swallowing uncooked eggs whole, and washing them down with deep fried Bombay duck. Grandfather died of a heart attack a month before I was born, leaving his pregnant daughter completely devastated and his new son-in-law with no time to make amends.

Mum's relations with her mother had never been cordial, but now they were on a head-on collision course. Grandma disowned her immediately, using the pretext that she had 'married out' and therefore had no right to anything that Grandfather had left behind. To show the world that although she had 'married out', she was every inch a woman of the day, she cut her hair short, had it 'permanently waved', and stopped wearing saris and Kolhapuri *chappals*. She switched to dresses and began to wear closed-heel shoes instead. Once again on the edge of penury, Mum stretched every rupee her husband earned. She now had *two* young children, a rented house on Ardeshir Irani Road in Poona, and a husband who was constantly getting himself into trouble at work.

We lived in Rita House until I was about six years old and my brother was at that lovely age of between four and five. A porcupine in the woods behind the house, a rat snake who coiled himself on the wrought iron spiral staircase that took you to Esme Aunty's house upstairs, a tap in the garden where I would often wash my feet and then slip and fall . . . these are my earliest memories of Rita House. Before we were shackled by kindergarten schedules, we went to Panchgani for breaks from the city in our forever new 1956 Vauxhall. It used to take us up to eight hours on the Khambatki and Pasarni Ghats with several stops in between to cool off the steaming engine. The long winding road would be lined with trees, and you could pass a whole hour without seeing a single other car on the road. Funnily enough, after all these years what I remember the most vividly about those road trips is the way everything smelled.

There was a strangely tarry smell when your engine stalled and you looked under the car for any oil leaks. When Dad popped the side flaps of the bonnet open, there would be the salty smell of the steam from the overworked radiator. When the engine needed cooling and we had to wait on the side of the road, there was the familiar swish of the grass mat that we would open out and spread for our family picnic. Roast chicken, mayonnaise, and chapattis were our standard picnic lunch. To save on washing up and also because we would need the pressure cooker when we got to Panchgani, Mum would roast the chicken in the cooker and carry the cooker without opening it once. This meant that opening the cooker was an act comparable to the last chapter of a murder mystery. Would it be well done? Would there be the brown greasy strips stuck to the bottom of the cooker? Would I get a share of the roast potato or would it go to my brother? Or, saddest of all sad thoughts, would it have been picked off the stove in a rush and had not come out golden brown and greasy? So many decades later, I can still taste the flavours of my mother's favourite 'road trip' meal.

Those flavours, her handing out pieces to us as we sat in a circle around her, the scent of the air and of the food, that to me is the scent of memories.

There used to be many road trips in those days. When we were little, Dad would bundle us into the car in our pyjamas, saying, '*Chalo, Panchgani wale!*' All aboard for the Panchgani road trip! We were obliged to take every vacation there just to claim our ownership rights. Mum had had to fight in a court of law for her inheritance after Grandpa died. Tehmina maintained that she, Rustomjee's widow, was the rightful heir and that as Rustomjee's widow she should have inherited all the properties, the monies in the banks, and whatever else. Grandpa had been a simple man. He was generous to a fault, giving friends and people lesser fortunate than he was monetary help without as much as a promissory note.

In his handwritten last will and testament in Gujarati, my grandfather had left everything he owned to his only daughter and had appointed Tehmina as the sole executor of the will. Grandma was livid. She fortified herself in Tehmi Terrace and barred us from entering the house. She then made a road trip to Panchgani and put a lock on the front door of the house there. Mum had no choice but to take the matter to court. A long and prolonged court case between mother and daughter took place in the High Court of Bombay. Family friends and neighbours were often entrusted with looking after us during tedious 'court dates'.

The court ruled in Mum's favour, and Mum repossessed her own house in Panchgani. For our school holidays in the summer, we could now go home to the land of red earth. The courts had also given us the full freedom to come and live in Tehmi Terrace whenever we wanted to. We were over the moon. Now there would be no more squeezing ourselves into Zenobia and Dara's pocket-sized balcony at Sea View Terrace in Khar for the night. There would be no visits to Freny Aunty and Dara Uncle's Shapur Baug flat while Mana and Pa were at the lawyers. We had our own home for our night halts.

We now had a house in Bombay. We assumed that we would have the full run of the nine bedrooms now that we owned it. Not so. Tehmina had barricaded herself on the first floor, taken in tenants on the ground floor, and we had to squeeze ourselves in the two rooms upstairs. She had heavy collapsible doors with a huge padlock on it, and even we, her own grandchildren, had to take an appointment to go see her. As age took her to a more mellowed state, she would allow us to run down the stairs and come and see her whenever we wanted to, but she still expected us to call out to her to announce our presence. Mum, however, was still on frosty terms with her mother, and Dad would insist on stuffing us with pork, salami, and sausages for breakfast every morning believing that it would 'ward off the evil eye' that our grandmother had undoubtedly cast on us. I still remember how we would have to call out, 'Grandmaaa! Graandma!' throughout the house as soon as we entered her floor.

Tehmi Terrace, the house in Mumbai

Grandma's floor was actually her entire universe. Our family of five and two dogs were squashed into two rooms and a bathroom upstairs, while Granny, by herself, without servant or dog, occupied five bedrooms, a servant's wing, three kitchens, and two long corridors. Whatever our parents' grudges might have been, they never let that influence our relationship. We just thought it all good fun. For it was worth it just to have a grandmother, a blood relation at last. I don't know how we survived those hot summer months in hothouse Bombay in those days. Year in and out, Grandma would not allow us to buy a fridge or install a telephone. It broke my mother's heart to see the house and her children suffer in the heat, and she kept her own spirits up by telling us stories of how the house in Bandra once buzzed with the chattering of servants and the clatter of imported china. They had even had a man call in every Sunday to wind up the old grandfather clocks in the house.

While Grandma lived alone in this large old house in Bandra, Mum and Dad, we three children and two dogs, lived in Baroda seven and a half hours away. For us, Grandma was someone with a lot of money while we had to subsist on a government salary. Yet, we were the ones having all the fun. We never worried about being kidnapped for ransom or murdered in our beds for our money. Poor rich Grandma wasn't so lucky. She feared every footfall that echoed in the great big house and screamed at every stranger who walked up to her door. Her confidantes were few; her friends none. Her only support was her sister's son, well into middle age himself but relatively agile. He helped her get around, and it was with him that she made her trips to lawyer's offices, accountants, and the High Court. At the end of the ten-year legal battle and sampling at Bombay's many new restaurants, he relieved her of over a hundred thousand rupees and left, his hopes of receiving everything she possessed dashed.

Grandma was not a tall woman. She was about four feet and six inches tall and had a pear-like shape. She always wore white, and her skin was softer than a baby's. She never feared laughter lines or wrinkles for she very rarely ever smiled. Mum said she used to bathe in milk once a week and had never let a bar of soap touch her face. She scrubbed herself with a paste of double cream and chickpea flour. I suppose the air in Bombay was not so polluted then. Grandma never trusted banks and never kept a bank account. Her room always looked like she was ready for a sea voyage. She kept all her cash packed in tin trunks or leather suitcases, luggage that you would normally see on board a ship. All the tins used to be stacked one on top of the other in a rather unstable pyramid in her room. Out of fear of being murdered for her money, she never allowed anyone in. A neighbour's daughter, Anisa, would come over from her dad's Mom & Pop store and look in to see how Grandma was. A clerk in a bank next door would come over to see if she needed any clerical work done.

Grandma Tehmina on her wedding day

When we visited, she would ask us to sit on a chair at a dining table under her baleful eye. Her table would be covered in old newspapers. We spent most of our mornings in Bandra reading Grandma's tablecloths. Bored after a while, we would then sit quietly waiting for some drama to unfold. Her driver Shankar would unfailingly provide the day's entertainment. He would stand at the doorway, swaying from side to side, and call out to her. Grandma would then answer him with some rather endearing swear words. That was his password. He would then enter the house, in a funny half-roll and half-walk, a few unstable steps at a time. She would then begin her screaming, asking him to walk a little faster to which he would reply with a few cuss words. His glazed eye would then try and focus on whatever she was trying to instruct him to do.

Old newspapers were not the only thing that covered the furniture and old wood-fired stoves in the house. There were also the eggshells. Grandma believed that empty unwashed eggshells repelled geckos without harming them. Every corner of the house, every window sill and ledge was covered in unwashed eggshells. The eggshells certainly worked, and there were no geckos in the house. In their place, there was a population boom of cockroaches and mosquitoes. The house smelled of mould, rising damp, and boiled cauliflower. Grandma had lived on *bhakras, popaljees,* and chicken patties and had only used her gas burners to heat up food that she would pick up from the Ratan Tata Institute.

Unwilling to hire help, Grandma had solved the problem of having problematic domestic help. She never drank tea or coffee unless we were there to wash up afterwards and only drank Duke's Raspberry instead of water. We were quite happy to do the same ourselves. There were no water bottles to be washed in Grandma's house and no water to be boiled and filled in clay pots like in our home in Baroda.

The Duke's truck would come around every Thursday, replacing the 'empties'. Grandma refused to buy a fridge and would not allow us to have one upstairs. Instead, Grandma had an icebox that kept drinks cold. Grandma's icebox was unique. It looked like a fancy wooden cupboard with her monogram TRP (Tehmina Rustomjee Patell) on the outside and had tin shelves with holes cut out in places on the inside. Ice blocks were delivered by a bullock cart every afternoon from the ice factory off Hill Road. This block was then put on the top and bottom shelves of the ice-box. Bottles of raspberry were then jammed into the middle shelf. Cold ice water dripped on to the bottles and kept our drinks cold.

Grandma's icebox

For more entertainment there was the Jasmine Club next door. Ladies in crisp cotton sarees or belted frocks would float into the club and settle in on chairs to play a round of cards in the club compound. I would watch them with envy, dreaming of opening a ladies' club myself someday. By a quirk of fate, I met the daughter of one of those card-playing ladies years later. She remembered how they used to sit out in the Jasmine Club garden playing cards and chatting about 'who was walking about with whom these days'. Her name was Dolly Shroff and she mentioned how *they* used to envy *us* living in such a great big house as Tehmi Terrace.

It was a delight to hear from her about the Bandra of the 1940s. Dolly remembered how a man servant would accompany her to school and back because the forest was so dense on Pali Hill because 'there were all kinds of loafers' lurking about. Grandma, despite what had transpired between

Mum and her, was also always warning us against 'layabouts and loafers'. A beautiful lady in her youth, she had apparently been kidnapped once by some agents of the Nizam of Hyderabad long before she had married Grandpa. Her kidnappers had kept her in someone's house, awaiting orders. The Nizam probably had some other distraction then and Grandma's kidnappers had let her go back to her uncle's in Nagpur. Had the Nizam been interested, our family history would have been something else.

XV

The Family Tree

'Siganpore chey gaamdu, hawamaan saaru, gamey tyarey padhaaru, nathi navai tyan taadi ni jaraaye, posswari piyun to pet dharye, reet sarni navjote karey jarthosti, aavjo sukhethi na visaru dosti.'

Six months after Mum passed away in early 2014, I found, amongst her papers, a brief history of her grandmother's story. Grandma Goolbai, she writes, was the second wife of Pallonji Dhunjibhai Patell and was born in Aden to a Burjorji Gustadji Lohraspa (Mody). Burjorji Lohraspa went to Aden some 200 years ago as a result of Islamic persecution in Iran. He decided to take the rather risky sea voyage out of Iran with his wife in a merchant sailing ship, not knowing where they were headed. Apparently, if the captain of the ship so desired he could drop them off at the first port in call. They landed in Aden and worked their way to India a little later in the year 1803. Fanciful as it sounds, this Burjorji Lohraspa was believed to be a direct descendant of Lohraspa, the persecuted ruler of Iran, often mentioned in the Zend Avesta, the sacred book of the Parsis.

Apparently, Burjorji started working in Aden in a shop. In a few years, he was able to buy up the small shop with his savings. The shop slowly turned into a provision store, selling British-made goods in Aden. The Indians in Aden began to address Burjorji as 'Mody' or Indian keeper of groceries. Burjorji and his wife had many sons and daughters, but there are no records of this family. We only know that his daughter Goolbai married Pallonji Patell, my mother's grandfather, a farmer from Siganpore near Surat. The Patell family tree can be traced as far back as a man named Karwa 'Jogi' who came on a boat with his wife and children to a small port named Desa on the Gujarat coast. They too suffered persecution in Iran and the family is said to have weathered some serious hardship.

The Jogis only survived because of the generosity and kindness of other families they met along the coast. It was the small merchants and their wives that gave them shelter and taught them how to trade along the shore to survive. Apparently, Karwa sang ballads in Farsi, and this talent made him very welcome in the traditions ports around Desa. He was nicknamed Jogi or Minstrel by his fellow traders. From here, he made his way to Pallanpur, worked the fields there, and gradually established a small grocery store there. This business grew, and he and his sons prospered. One of Karwa's sons, Manji, came to Siganpore village near Surat and built what my mother called the *gaam nu gher,* the village house.

The Patell family tree then tells us that Manji and his descendants ploughed land in the village as serfs at first. They gradually bought lands in and around the village and also had a small village shop. It was during the British East India Company settlement in Surat that the little store in Siganpore flourished and his friend Manekji Mody, encouraged Pallonji to accompany him to Aden. Siganpore still remained his ancestral village, but his work shifted to Aden. It was much later that Pallonji and Manekji's sister Goolbai were to marry each other in Aden. It was Pallonji's second marriage, Goolbai's first.

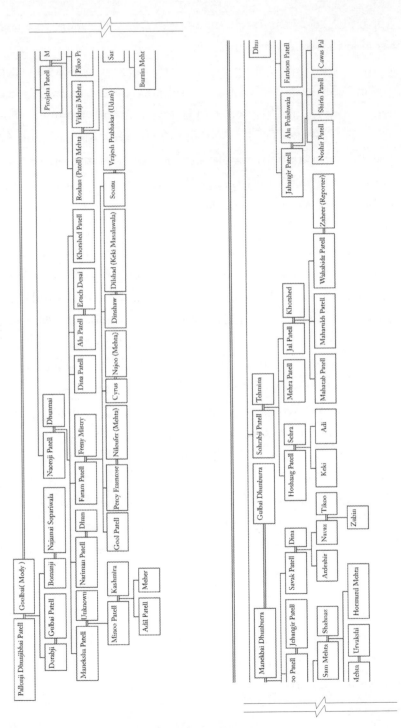

The Patell family tree

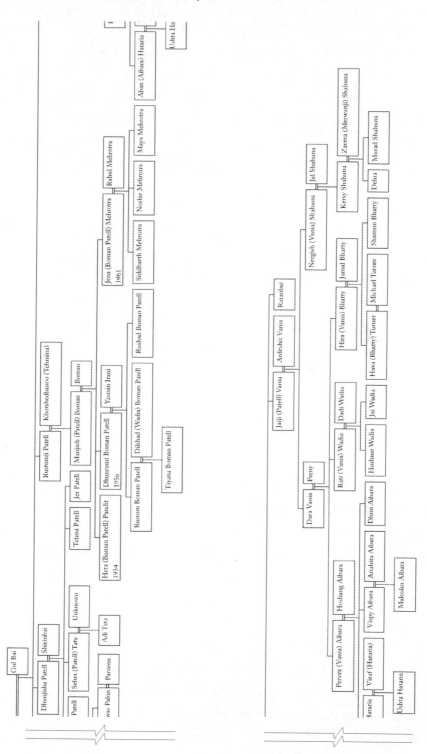

Pallonji's first job in Aden was that of a bottle washer and 'filler'. He often faced snide remarks behind his back and was referred to as *battli bharoo*, bottle filler as he worked on the British-made soda water machines. These glass bottles broke frequently while he worked, and Pallonji would come home often with his hands bleeding. He switched jobs and began to work at the Burjorji Gustadji Stores owned by the fiery-tempered and golden-hearted Manekji's father Burjorji. He must have done well here and was soon married to Burjorji's petite and soft-spoken daughter Goolbai after the death of his first wife Dinbai.

We know very little about Dinbai. We do know, however, that Pallonji had two sons, Dorabjee and Bomanjee by his first wife Dinbai, and Goolbai undertook to look after them. Later she herself had five boys and two girls, making it a family of seven boys and two girls. They traded in rice, spices, and food grains and covered South Africa, Ethiopia, and Abyssinia even delving into the ivory trade when the opportunity presented itself. More members of the family, including Pallonji's father Dhunjibhai (or Dhunjibhoy), joined the business, and it became the norm to marry into the family to ensure that the wealth stayed within the family core circle. We hear that Burjorji retired from active business in Aden and came to Poona and became something of a social activist for the Parsis of Poona.

When the Pallonjee Dhunjibhai family completed fifty years in Aden in the January 1914, they returned to India for a 'Golden Jubilee' celebration held in the then tiny village of Siganpore to the crisp mansion that was now eleven years old. The large mansion had been modestly named Patell Cottage. In the absence of men in the house, Pallonjee's unmarried daughter Ratanbai had designed and built the house in 1903, Queen Victoria's Jubilee Year. Today Siganpore is part of the Surat Municipal Corporation limits, but in 1914, things were different. On account of the wealth they had acquired and the lands they owned and farmed in the village, they were given the title of village *patels*, headmen. The title soon became a name and to distinguish the Parsi *patels* from the Gujarati *patels* in the village, this family attached an extra 'l'. After all, they were an important family. They had a British connection.

The house in the village

From the brochures specially printed for the occasion, it is apparent that the seven brothers and two sisters were close. A *jasan*, sacred blessing, had been organised for the occasion, and there was much food and drink and many speeches extolling the virtues and the wealth of this family. Rice, mangoes, tamarind, jackfruit, wood apples, fresh from the farms, were given away as gifts. The *jasan* invitation had a picture of the row houses in Aden, the provision store that had brought prosperity to the family and the house in Siganpore. The other images are captioned 'Pier-Aden', 'Dar-e-Meher Aden', and 'Patell Cottage'.

About the village in which they all grew up, Sohrabjee Pallonjee Patell writes, '*Siganpore chey gaamdu, hawamaan saaru, gamey tyarey padhaaru, nathi navai tyan taadi ni jaraaye, posswari piyun to pet dharye, reet sarni navjote karey jarthosti, aavjo sukhethi na visaru dosti*', which he apparently sang to an appreciative audience at the celebratory function. Roughly translated, this song begins with a dedication to the salubrious village of Siganpore and welcomes everyone to the village. It says that fresh toddy from the coconut palm is no novelty and that even if you have a little bit, it gives you immense satisfaction. Here, it says, every Zoroastrian has been initiated into the religion in the proper orthodox manner and that friendships are never forgotten.

The reverse of the invitation carries the names of all Pallonjee Dhunjibhoy's sons – Dorabjee, Bomanjee, Navrojjee, Pirojshaw, Sohrabjee, Dhunjeeshaw, and Rustomjee and the names of all the grandsons with their first initials as clues to their fathers' names. Manekjee N, Jehangir N, Nariman N, Shavakshaw P, Jal S, Hoshang S, Jehangir D. Manijeh; Rustomjee's only child did not figure anywhere in the invitation as did not any of Pallonjee's daughters, daughters-in-law, or granddaughters. None of the ladies of the house have been mentioned in the family tree that goes back nine generations. That, apparently, was the custom. Girls did not count.

It was fashionable then to recall one's humble beginnings. At the Golden Jubilee function, Pallonjee wanted everyone to know this. He also wanted all his invitees to know how eminent a citizen he had now become. There is a long list of posts he had held.

1870 – Manager, Messrs Muncherjee Eduljee & Sons, Aden

1878 – Partner, Messrs Muncherjee Eduljee & Sons, Aden

1879 – Partner, Messrs Muncherjee Dhunjeebhoy & Co., Aden

1890 – Proprietor, Messrs Pallonjee Dinshaw & Co., Aden

1896 – Trustee, Parsi Anjuman Funds, Aden

1891 – Trustee, The Prince of Wales Dispensary, Aden

1892 – Trustee, The Parsee Anjuman Funds, Siganpore

1911 – Proprietor, Dinshaw Cawasjee & Co., Aden
1911 – Trustee, The Muktad Funds, Vesu, Surat

And at the age of sixty-eight, in 1912 – Trustee, The Bai Pirojbai Girls School, Surat

We also know that one of his sons sang a rather sycophantic poem to his illustrious father. The song went something like this: '*Pagey pari karun prathna enaji raho, harsh vadhe chey joi maata ney saaji, maata pita icchu umar dasji, Pallonjee purush paramathi uch*'. Through the heavy mist of filial love and aged paper all one can read of this poem is the dedication of a son (or several sons) to parents that they consider worthy of worship. The poem also says how their happiness and joy brims over on seeing their parents, that they would like to add on their years to their parents' and that Pallonjee is a cut above the rest. Amen.

Afterword

What is it that makes us do certain things in life? What is it that compels us to take those decisions that become our life's turnstiles and, in turn, affect our life and the lives of others? Ask someone famous, and they will tell you they were inspired by this one or that book, a great person, or a good book. Every decision I have taken, leaving home in India to go to the UK for 'further studies', chucking up the college in Birmingham, and trotting down to London to work as a barmaid, on a photocopying machine, as a tea girl in a factory, then landing up in Tanzania, East Africa, working as Dr Jane Goodall's field and research assistant, coming back to India after a childhood romance and subsequent marriage that went wrong, joining an advertising firm and then ending up working full time for an environmental group in Mumbai, serving as honorary secretary for a heritage protection NGO and then leaving Mumbai for Munnar, Kerala, meeting with a biking accident there and landing in Goa, staying there for twenty years, setting up a heritage NGO, being awarded a Homi Bhabha Fellowship to study the work of the master builders of Goa, and then coming back, full circle, to Mumbai to look after my ailing mother, and perhaps to write my memoirs.

None of these decisions were inspired. None of these decisions were the result of reading a good book or meeting a great personality. They were simply taken because I had no choice. There was no other way to survive. Why did I have to go to the UK? My mother wanted me to. In her mind, that was the only way I could be separated from my childhood sweetheart and so she sent me off to the University of Birmingham, 'to widen my horizons, broaden the mind, and meet some new people'. The separation deepened my resolve. I landed at the university, stayed there for three whole miserable days, and trotted down to London to live with friends in their box room at twenty-five pounds a week. I saved all the tuition money that my mother had set aside for my education and worked alternately as barmaid, tea girl, basement photocopying machine operator to be able to save enough to send my childhood sweetheart a ticket to a new future together. I did save enough for a ticket but the rest never happened as planned. Thanks to a combination of the sweetheart's foolhardiness and tough British Immigration Laws, he was not allowed to enter the country. We were compelled to leave. And ever since, it has been a series of compulsions and pressures that have given way to reactions and responses, never once giving me the opportunity to think about what I really want out of life.

And you thought this was a book about being part of a heritage protection movement? Or the story of the four houses that I've inherited? Why so many personal details then? Well, just to illustrate my point that everything you do is the result of some personal pressure or some family or financial compulsion. And that if the world around you recognises this as some kind of achievement, then that achievement is simply a by-product of this 'no choice' decision. For example, how did I come to found a heritage protection group in Goa, of all places? How did I end up writing seven books on Goan heritage, publishing some of them and becoming something of an acknowledged expert on Goan heritage? I did not plan or orchestrate any of this, and neither can I truthfully say that 'oh, opportunities came my way'. I just had to do what I did to survive.

About the Author

Heta Pandit, born 25 August 1954, has a Master's Degree in Statistics, Economics, and Mathematics from the MS University of Baroda, Gujarat, India. She has worked with world renowned ethologist Dr Jane Goodall at a chimpanzee research station in Tanzania, East Africa for four years before returning to Mumbai, India, to work with the Bombay Environmental Action Group and Indian Heritage Society, Bombay Chapter. Ms Pandit has worked in the field of heritage conservation and other related fields for over twenty-eight years since that time. She has also served on the Heritage Conservation Committee in Bombay (now Mumbai) under the Chairmanship of Mr Jamshed Kanga, former Commissioner of MCGB.

As a freelance journalist and resident of Goa, she has researched and written extensively on the conservation and architecture of the houses of Goa. She has several articles and stories on the subject of heritage conservation to her credit. Her book titled *Houses of Goa*, co-authored by architect Ms Annabel Mascarenhas, was published in July 1999 and sold over 4,500 copies in India and abroad. The next book *A Heritage Guide to Kerala* won her an award from the Kerala Government in the year 2000. She was felicitated by the prestigious Menezes Braganza Institute, Panaji,

Goa, for her contribution to Goan literature through her short stories and translations from the Marathi to the English in March 2000 with a title *Lekhika 2000*.

She has subsequently written several books titled *Dust and Other Short Stories from Goa*, *Walking in Goa*, *In and Around Old Goa*, *Hidden Hands – The Master Builders of Goa*, and *Walking with Angels*, an architectural treatise on the churches of Goa. She is currently working on a book titled *Goa Style* that showcases restored heritage houses and home owners that have infused their own ethnic cultures into those Goan houses.

Ms Pandit also writes short stories in which she makes an attempt to highlight the plight of subaltern groups in Goan society. She also translates fiction from the Marathi into the English language. Her fictional writing and translations display a deep understanding of subaltern Goan society. She has designed several walking tours in Goa for the benefit and education of visitors to Goa. Ms Pandit founded an NGO based in Goa and dedicated to building awareness on Goan heritage named the Goa Heritage Action Group. For the years 1998–2000, Ms Pandit was awarded a Homi Bhabha Fellowship to study the work of the master builders of Goa, a subaltern group of artisans and craftsmen responsible for the creation of the beautiful heritage houses of Goa.

Ms Pandit comes from a family of Indian Parsi Zoroastrains, migrants to India from Iran. This book is a personal history of the houses she owns in Mumbai, Panchgani, and Goa in India interwoven with the stories of several generations. The book, therefore, is not just about houses but also a capsule on social history at a micro level. It is also a reflection of the eccentricities and quirks of this extraordinary community and their adaptation to the social and cultural customs in the land of their adoption. At a micro level, Ms Pandit has lived an extraordinary life. She has worked as world-renowned ethologist Dr Jane Goodall's field and research assistant in Tanzania; was India's first woman tea planter, and has advocated and pioneered several preservation campaigns for the severely threatened historic buildings of her country. This is her story.

Glossary of Non-English Words and Phrases

(In alphabetical order)

Agiary – Parsi Fire Temple, a temple open only to members of the Zoroastrian faith in India

Avanti – welcome or come in (Italian)

Banianis – derogatory for Indian in Africa, a corruption of Bania or shopkeeper

Batasas – savoury baked cookies made with ghee, flour salt and cumin seed

Baug – a gated colony for the exclusive residential use of Parsis in Bombay usually managed by a family trust or the Bombay Parsi Panchayat

Bawa – derogatory term for a Parsi (man) in India

Bawaji ka beta – derogatory for a Parsi child, literally a Parsi son

Bhakras – Parsi deep-fried sweet snack resembling a doughnut

Biryani – spicy rice usually made with meat or chicken

Boma – community living in Africa often a series of huts built in a concentric circle

Burun pão – round crusty bread that is soft on the inside

Chalk na dabba – traditional stencil tins used to decorate the floor in a Parsi home, an offshoot of the Hindu auspicious decorations called *rangoli*

Chappals – Indian open sandals

Chikki – brittle made with unrefined sugar and nuts

Dhal – lentil soup, India's staple usually eaten with rice or *rotis*

Dasturji – Zoroastrian priest, the *ji* being a respectful suffix

Entrada – entrance (Portuguese)

Gaadi samaan – car stuff

Garas – an embroidered saree originally from China but later produced in
India exclusively for Parsis

Garba – a traditional dance from Gujarat performed in a ring during the
Navratri (Nine Nights) festival

Gully – a lane or street

Jalebis – an Indian extrusion sweet made with rice flour and saturated in
sugar syrup

Jasan – Parsi blessing ceremony that can be held in a home or fire temple

Kathas – stories from the Indian epics, literally stories

Mali – gardener

Mamu – an endearment for your mother's brother

Mehfils – gatherings of people interested in poetry, philosophy, and music

Murabbas – jam made from mangoes or squashes, pumpkins, etc.

Navjotes – initiation ceremony for Zoroastrian children usually performed
prior to puberty

Nimboos – lemons (Hindi)

Papads – also called *poppadoms*, flat fritters made from lentil flour usually
an accompaniment to a meal

Parjaats – Parsi Gujarati for someone who is not a Parsi

Parotta – flat unleavened bread in India usually cooked on a flat griddle

Popaljees – Parsi sweet snack made with fermented dough

Puja – votive offering to a deity, a ritual

Qawalis – community singing in two competitive groups often dedicated
to the divine

Rajma – red beans, a North Indian staple

Rotis – unleavened light Indian bread

Sadhus – an Indian spiritual usually a man

Samaan – stuff, a generic all-encompassing term

Samosas – an Indian deep-fried savoury snack, usually a pocket of dough with potato or meat stuffing

Sapat – flat leather slippers, probably a Chinese import brought to India by the Parsis, the name is from the original Portuguese for footwear *sapatas*

Sattvik – bland food devoid of onions, garlic, spices believed to suppress the tempers

Sorpotel – spicy Goan sausage dish

Thalis – Indian-style steel plates

Ugali – maize meal in East Africa, also *mealie* in South Africa

Unani – Indian term for ancient Greek medicine as adapted by Indian medical practitioners

Vaddo – ward, a smaller administrative division in a village in Goa

Printed in the United States
By Bookmasters